NANCY HALE was born in Boston, Massachusetts, in 1908, and was educated at the School of the Museum of Fine Arts in Boston. After studying in her father's studio for a number of years, she became an assistant editor at *Vogue*, then *Vanity Fair*, and later was the first woman reporter for *The New York Times*. She has written over fifty short stories for the *New Yorker*, and has been a frequent contributor to *Harper's*, *Harper's Bazaar*, *Virginia Quarterly Review*, *Scribner's*, *Saturday Evening Post*, and other publications. Her numerous full-length works of fiction and nonfiction include THE YOUNG DIE GOOD, A NEW ENGLAND GIRLHOOD, MARY CASSATT (biography), and THE PRODIGAL WOMEN, a Literary Guild Selection that was translated into German, French, and Swedish, and will soon appear in an Avon edition. A winner of the O'Henry short story prize, Nancy Hale is married to a distinguished scholar and editor, and makes her home in Charlottesville, Virginia.

THE LIFE
IN THE STUDIO

Nancy Hale

 A DISCUS BOOK/PUBLISHED BY AVON BOOKS

All of the chapters in this book except "The Black Cape," "Grape Jelly" and "Journeys" appeared originally in *The New Yorker*.

"The Black Cape" appeared in the *Ladies Home Journal* under the title "My Mother's Clothes."

"Journey's" appeared originally in *Virginia Quarterly Review*.

AVON BOOKS
A division of
The Hearst Corporation
959 Eighth Avenue
New York, New York 10019

First Discus Printing, July, 1980

DISCUS TRADEMARK REG. U.S. PAT. OFF. AND IN
OTHER COUNTRIES, MARCA REGISTRADA, HECHO EN
U.S.A.

Printed in the U.S.A.

To John C. Coleman

Foreword

When, after my mother died, I started to write the story about clearing out her studio with which this collection begins, it never occurred to me I was writing about anything more than that. Only much later, working on the subsequent stories — which came to concern my father also, whose studio I cleared out when *he* died more than thirty years ago — did it dawn on me that those artists' studios were less my subject than another, less tangible region I was never able to clear out while they were still alive. My father's studio, which was rented, really did have to be cleared out, but my mother's didn't. She, a lot tidier person than I any day, never felt the compulsion to sort its accumulation of the possessions of several generations. With me it had felt like an irresistible instinct, a profound duty.

Then, in that curious way outward events do come to cluster around a new state of one's mind, I began getting letters about clearing out. A New Mexico friend wrote, after the death of her mother, "I am going through the accumulation of years and years . . . all those things she could never bear to throw away. How essential to clear one's decks, if only for the children." And another friend, on the other side of the world: "Reading and disposing of my father's letters is like following the thread of Ariadne. I only hope to God in the end it's going to lead out of this labyrinth." Half my friends suddenly appeared to be busy with a preoccupation I had supposed private to me.

Many of them mentioned the sensation I'd had myself, like a deep ground-swell, of realignment after the final loss, no matter how late in life, of both parents. I was an only child; but even friends who had brothers and sisters spoke of feeling left, stark alone, to head up the old mystic triangle. We also seemed to share the more heartless feeling of being at last free of the past. But the past is at least as hard to get shed of as the contents of those lesser repositories, artists' studios.

That indispensable ideal, living in the present with one's sights set on the future, has come for some people to imply extirpation of the past. Artists, for all their impracticality, would recognize such a notion as impractical, not to say uncreative. With their instinct for making something, artists tend to respect the past as something also made. Uneasily aware that the future is where death is waiting, artists find its balance in the past, and the life there — well versed in how protean the supposedly dead past can be, how with change of attitude it can alter from curse into blessing and back again; from trap into escape hatch. The artist's experience is that, in art, ideas of past and present, life and death achieve a transformed union analogous to the present.

Among those who are trapped in today it is hard to tell who gets the wilder misconceptions of past and future — the young about their elders or older people about the young; the living have so little room to view each other with objectivity. Sometimes only after death has introduced its regretful perspective are the vast, Easter Island masks that gazed down on one's childhood seen for what they really were all the time; not darkly, but face to face. The old, bleak villains, the heroes, the pariahs are still, if one is lucky, transformable into whatever their real truth was. Else a great inheritance — the only inheritance one has a right to — lies accumulated in the repositories of one's forebears' lives, unreclaimed.

This book is about the artists I grew up among — my mother, my father, my aunt. Succeeding chapters in the volume, although they tell stories on them such as about my mother's run-in with Freud, the Harvard-Yale game my father took me to, the fateful noon whistle on the ocean liner, also in a way concern things I unearthed in clearing out their studios; for these later stories too surprised me by turning out to reveal secrets I didn't know I knew. What I am trying is to clue the reader in on the game any number can play, of looking into a mirror that reflects looking into a mirror that reflects. Down at the far end I hope what will be seen is not death at all, but the life in the studio.

Contents

ONE

Family Ties

What Haunts Thee in Fond Shapes

COMMON sense, cleanliness, and my advisers tell me I should get this old studio by the sea — which my aunt built, and where she and other artists painted and made etchings on a press set up under the skylight, where my mother painted for years after she inherited it — cleared out and turned into an ordinary room with a big north window that I can use in everyday life.

All this accumulation is of no immediate use to anyone alive today. "All this junk," my husband calls it, as he views the half-empty pots of glue and linseed oil and turpentine; the balsa-wood plane models, broken, my son made while my mother was painting him; coils of wire used on boats for some purpose; cigar boxes of dried-up paint tubes;

the conch shells in the still-life composition that was the last thing my mother painted before she died; the rotted leather trunks full of photographs mounted on cards in the Victorian manner, of ladies in bustles, gentlemen with beards, once somebody's friends but now forever unknown; a yellow luster vase; a pair of desiccated rubber gloves for handling the etching plates in an acid bath; a pile of old *Transactions* of the Brontë Society; several palettes, still set, the blobs of paint dried as hard as multicolored marbles; plaster casts, damaged, of Aphrodite, of a della Robbia *bambino,* of an *écorché* — a model of the nude stripped to show the muscles; a pile of oil pochades my father painted on one of his infrequent visits away from his Boston studio, of apple blossoms against the sea; several cheap campstools for outdoor painting, and several sketching easels, but no two of them in the same place; a small, heavy box labeled "Black sand found in Philip's room, 1900"; three nineteenth-century traveling desks — mahogany boxes whose inner writing surfaces, covered in velvet, are broken off the hinges; a cabinet whose shelves are entirely filled with shoeboxes, some empty, some filled with wire, with nails, with the wooden keys used in stretching canvases, with still more photographs of forgotten people, or, actually, with shoes, marked on the outside of the box, by my mother, disarmingly, "White Suade Sandles"; a number of wicker end tables, Victorian, that my mother found useful in setting up still-life; part of an ancestor's classical library, behind glass, its leather flaking off; a boxful of unremarkable minerals collected a hundred years ago by a little boy who died when he was ten; a china cabinet crowded with china, all of it broken, including the china pitcher, handle missing, that my father and his brothers' supper milk was poured from and that reads, in white china lettering:

> *What though my cates be poor?*
> *Take them in good part.*
> *May you have better cheer*
> *But not with better heart,*

and the low brown wooden table where they played games in the evenings, on one side of which some disgruntled little boy carved "Fat Paunch"; old letter file upon old letter file containing nothing but clippings from newspapers, of photographs that gave one of those now dead artists an idea for a composition; an enormous wooden bowl with packets of seed in it that are anywhere from ten to fifty years old and unquestionably sterile by now (if you pick up a handful at random, the labels read, in handwriting, "Oct. 1932 Black-Eyed Susans, original seed from E. Stewardson," or "Dill 1923," or "1940. Datura. Angel's Trumpet," or, in commercial print, "Okra — Dreer's Little Gem"); three sets of mortar and pestle; broken lamps; broken chairs; baskets filled with bits of old twine; a knitting bag that was once an oatmeal carton and that was covered in wallpaper, at summer camp, by my son for a September birthday present for his great-aunt; three tall racks intended to hold drawings and etchings that belonged to the aunt who built the studio.

"Clear it all out quick," my husband advises. "Then you'll have it off your mind. You did that with your father's studio." I did. I cleared out the Boston studio in two weeks when my father died, because it seemed important to get out of it before the lease expired. But it's hard to believe that is the right thing to do now.

All studios, because they have no formal arrangement the way a dining room or a living room has, tend to become repositories. Thirty years ago when I cleared my father's studio so quickly, I was searching for the certificates to some American Telephone & Telegraph stock my father had owned that were not in his safe-deposit box. I found one certificate under the bathtub, one in a 1914 *Saturday Evening Post,* two in the fireplace that was used to store maulsticks, rolls of unused canvas, and sketching easels, and one that had slipped through the floorboards of the model stand, but some never did turn up, and we had to apply to have new ones issued. Some other objects crowding my father's studio were probably valuable, some totally worthless, but I don't remember what they were now, because in the hurry to move out I got rid of everything.

There is no problem about what to do with some of the things in this studio by the sea. The Coromandel screen would be an adornment to any living room. The amateurish painting by my grandfather, Edward Everett Hale, properly a writer and clergyman, of Boston Common in the thirties of the last century, was assessed higher than anything in the house at the time an inventory was made for death taxes. The table all the boxes of paints are piled on is real Chippendale, the assessor said, besides being a good, useful table. The family letters can be given to a library that wants them. The dozens upon dozens of paintings and drawings by my mother can join the paintings by my father and my aunt up in the attic, which will then be so full that if anybody more in this family becomes an artist he will have to build a new studio in order to have a place to store his work in when *he* dies.

But what to do about ten or twelve big sheets of glass, intended to cover drawings but broken, cracked, or chipped? "Cut them in half and use them on smaller pictures," my son advises. But think of the work! The expense! What am I going to do with all my son's school papers that my mother saved — spelling and arithmetic and geography papers? "Throw them out, for heaven's sake," he says. Or with the finest of the writing desks, Chinese, inlaid with gold and mother-of-pearl, its hinges broken and lacquer dried and cracked? "Get it mended," someone says. But where, nowadays? Or with seventeen palm-leaf fans — some real palm leaves, some only shaped like palms, of paper, with charming Japanese wash drawings on them. Or a doll's tester bed with, lying on top of it, a doll's crinoline — bed broken, crinoline eaten by moths. Or the books my grandfather read as a child — *Harry and Lucy, The Sock Stories,* by Aunt Fanny, *Aesop's Fables,* all without covers, the bare leaves bound with rotting thread and crumbling glue?

I respect what my advisers, objective as I cannot be, recommend; but at the thought of taking hold of all this complicated assembly and throwing it out I quail. Even to imagine beginning to is like opening, in a dream, a nightmare closet upon confusion. I feel I can't.

What am I to do with yards of Irish lace, with boxes and boxes full of scraps of material, almost every one of them speaking of a real time, a real place? There is some checked brown gingham from my first bought dress (my mother made my clothes until I was thirteen). There is gray linen from the high-waisted frock I was wearing at school the day I leaned against a pine tree at recess and got pitch in my hair. There is a bit of the red-and-blue plaid smock my mother wore to paint in forty years ago, and of her brown silk afternoon dress that had a Binche lace collar, and of one of my grandmother's — her mother's — black brocade dresses, and her lavender satin mantle. There are several pieces of taffeta, pale cream color with a blue stripe running through it, that I was told when I was a child was French and part of a great-aunt's hoopskirt. In other days women used to make patchwork out of scraps like these, so that forever after or until the quilt disintegrated you could lean over and with a forefinger pick out your life's history from bits of a familiar dress, upholstery from a sheltering chair. Perhaps my mother, who could do anything with her hands, had some wild dream of fitting patchwork into her countless other accomplishments. But I shall never make patchwork. What am I going to do with all the pieces?

Possibly I am letting myself be too much affected by what are only material possessions. But I'd always thought of material possessions as having a monetary value. These objects seem more ineffable than material, like voices. At their realest, they are objects of virtue, keys to release the life that trembles behind them in the void and that I otherwise would never have suspected was there. It is as if you whirled around very quickly and caught the furniture in a room up to something; or as if, by a trick, you had at last been able to catch the uncatchable — the blind spot in your vision where anything can happen.

How can I throw away an anecdote about Winston Churchill and Sir Alexander Fleming, written out in quadruplicate, which I remember, suddenly, an uncle on my mother's side telling me, years ago? What I had no idea of was that he cared so about it. Now I see him sitting at his desk in Westchester County, the Benares brass lamp standing beside him, copying it out over and over for the friends he was going to give it to, send it to. Can he have made even *more* than four copies of this not very fascinating story? Am I to throw away a tiny emerald-green glass bottle, etched in gold, the broken stopper wedged in, that fits into a tiny chamois-leather case? The smelling salts are still visible, locked inside. If I worked on its stopper long enough I might be able to catch a whiff, but if I throw it out in the trash I know that I will never think of it again — or of the other case, black leather, that lies beside it. This case is like one of those miraculous snowstorm paperweights, in that it seems to contain a world. Inside it, a square glass, bevel-edged, for drinking out of, contains a metal spoon, a metal fork, and a penknife, all folded back neatly upon themselves to fit the glass that fits the case. Who did *that* belong to? Was it meant for carrying aboard a boat? Was it for camping?

So many of these objects do seem worlds in themselves, worlds I can at least peer into if I hold them in my hand. There is a collection of Victorian metal objects (brass? copper? they are black with time). One is an inkwell. You can tell it is an inkwell because there is an ink-stained china cup inside. The inkwell is in the shape of what I think must be a hut for savages. The round house itself is woven of strips (osiers? as in *Swiss Family Robinson?*), and its roof of reeds that point upward and are gathered into a bunch at the top. The hut has a sort of extension, a round sub-hut, whose roof you lift to dip your pen into the ink. But is it a hut? Here, on the "ground" outside it, is a huge metal fly. He is formed perfectly; is he also to scale? If he's to scale, then it can't represent a hut for savages, or at least it must be a hut for the most elfin of savages. Or *what* is it? There is no use trying to interest a collector in it, to find out. The roof is broken, the china cup inside is broken, and collectors only want perfect specimens. Everything in this whole studio is broken. But, as I have always been told, nobody is perfect.

"If you don't look out, you'll find yourself living in the past," a disapproving cousin says. "I loved them all, too, but it's so *sad,* to think about them now they're dead. Come on to the beach."

After she is gone I go on looking through a big pile of papers spilled on the floor in one corner, behind the Coromandel screen. Lots of them are just more pictures from newspapers that my mother clipped out, that gave her an idea. But what idea was she trying to capture? A young girl standing before a window, her hair a blaze from the sunshine behind her — that's easy. So is a photograph from *Vanity Fair* of the actress Grace George, posed in profile, a plume falling from her hat and around the curve of her neck. A brown rotogravure-section picture of the Egyptian architect Ti is less so. It is just very stiff, very archaic, very Egyptian. What *can* my mother have wanted to use that idea for, in a picture?

All at once I come on a whole batch, a dozen or more, of

photographs taken of this house when it was being built in 1911. I never knew before that they existed. Pictures of the granite for the house being quarried out of its own cellar, of the scaffolding, of the master mason laying the courses of stone, of the derrick, of the landscape as it then was, beyond the open construction.

My aunt engaged the mason, an old Swede, to build the house to suit his own ideas, because, she said, she wanted it to look like a North European farmhouse. I'd entirely forgotten his name, but now, as I squint at the snapshots of him, in his felt hat and shapeless sweater against that scenery which looks so curiously bare, I remember it was Jungquist, Alec Jungquist, and that the bushes and young trees used to be kept down by the pasturing of cows that belonged to Mr. Seppala, a Finn. The cows roamed the point, the moors, all summer. At night you could hear their cowbells tinkling in the fog.

Jungquist built most of the granite houses around here. Before his day the masons weren't up to it, and afterward granite houses cost too much. He had the independence of the Scandinavian, and when his wife died and he lived all alone he did everything for himself, including — when he realized he had a cancer in his throat — operating on it with a straight razor. He died, of course, of blood poisoning.

Gradually, as I turn over others in the mass of papers, I begin to notice the noise the flies of noonday make, as they buzz and bat against the big, high studio window, too high to be washed, where spiders have their webs; one can lie for hours on the old lumpy chaise longue, that is covered in faded blue denim, and watch the flies getting caught, struggling sometimes for a whole day, expiring, in the extensive and high-powered operations the spiders conduct up there. I get up from the floor where I have been sitting, stretch, and go to another window, the low one that overlooks the sea through the locusts' lacy foliage.

There lies the cove — glassy still, green, warm, shining, the way I love it. The granite point beyond is rosy in the sun. At this hour, all my friends are down there swimming. *Love calls us to the things of this world,* I repeat to myself as I go to change into my suit. True, but then what do you call what I feel for all this junk, these worlds?

Eyes and No Eyes, or,
The Art of Seeing

WHEN my father got home from his Boston studio just before dinner at night, he would go at once to my mother's studio, on the north side of our house in Dedham, and see how her day's work had progressed.

"I need a crit!" she would cry, embracing him at the front door. The slang abbreviation, used by callow art students, carried certain nuances that, as a child growing up in that house, I was sensitive to. It suggested the relationship of master and pupil, and this in turn suggested an attitude of respect on my mother's part, which, while deeply sincere, was also a delicate and needed attention. My father, besides teaching anatomy and life drawing, was an art critic of note and phenomenally informed on art in general, but was not so successful a painter as my mother. When I was a child, she had more portrait orders than she could fill, and her prices were steadily rising. My father supported the household on his salary from the Boston Museum School; the money my mother earned was put carefully away in order to provide for an old age that, alas, since my father died at sixty-six, they never shared.

She was always successful, right from the start. My father told me with pride how, at the openings of exhibitions of even her earliest genre paintings and those charcoal drawings for which she had developed a sharpened-point technique wholly her own, one Boston dealer used to put up a velvet cord across the entrance until the cream of the buying cream had had a preliminary view. When the cord was taken down, every picture in the show would have been sold. Another dealer often used to say to her, "I can sell anything you do." By the time I was ten, my mother had become largely engaged in the painting of portraits. Certain intramural mysteries — the private jokes, the secret language of portrait painters — I picked up (in that village of commuting stockbrokers and bankers) the way a little Christian child in pagan Rome might have picked up the trick of how to draw fish in the sand with his toe.

My father would stand in the white-walled room — lamplit around half past six in the evening, or, if the season was summer, in the strong light of day — backing away from the canvas on the big easel and coming up close again to indicate with his thumb something he felt needed fixing. He was heavyset, with a walrus mustache that half concealed his mouth. He had a way of letting his hand drop to his side with a hard slap after making such an indication. Since he carried loose kitchen matches in his pocket to light his pipe with, at least once, in his life class, a student had timidly to say, "Mr. Hale, there's smoke coming out of your pocket."

My mother sat on her high painting stool, her chin propped on her fist, paying rapt attention; she looked like a Pre-Raphaelite damozel leaning out from the gold bar of Heaven; the room they were in was small and square. It had been just an ordinary room, until its whole north wall was replaced by windows, with short sash curtains that enabled my mother to make innumerable adjustments in the exact degree of that essential to painting as she knew it — the light.

On dark days she always called off a portrait sitting. She said she couldn't see anything when it was dark. Her eyes were certainly very different from lay eyes. When she and I went out shopping together, I could peer into the dark recesses behind a shopwindow and make out all sorts of objects — loaves of bread or garden rakes or magazines or whatever we might be looking for — while my mother, confronted by anything in deep shadow, would all her life simply say, "I can't see a thing."

One of her great artistic coups was inventing for herself a way of doing charcoal drawings of scenes in the falling snow — church spires, farmhouses, heavy-laden pines, which she indicated only as dark forms, leaving white paper for snow. These drawings were among the most sought-after examples of her work. On bitter, blizzardy winter mornings when my father and I would leave the house to walk to the village, a mile away, he to the train and I to school, he would re-

mark, "Well, there's one comfort. She'll get something wonderful out of this."

When he was giving a criticism of one of my mother's portraits, he was likely to end up by saying, "Well! How do
they like it?" Then they would laugh and make awful faces
at each other.

But it was not always a laughing matter. Sometimes my
mother was driven to despair by an objection a sitter, or a sitter's family, had made. "You know what Mr. G—— said? 'I
can't exactly say why, but somehow that just isn't my Mar-
garet.'" She used the mocking tones in which, in our family,
laymen were quoted.

"'A portrait's a picture with something the matter with
the mouth,'" my father would say, quoting Sargent.

Faced with real live laymen, my mother was very timid
and anything but mocking. Sometimes this got her into trouble. A Mrs. W—— had ordered a portrait of herself, and
Mrs. W——'s domineering old mother insisted that her
daughter sit in a favorite pale-blue chiffon evening dress
with a pale-blue feather boa. "She looks so awful in it," my
mother told my father. "Like a glass of skim milk. I don't
see it that way."

"Just tell them so," my father advised. "Tell them you
can't see it. You can't paint what you can't see."

My mother couldn't tell them so, however, and when the
portrait of the blond, blue-eyed Mrs. W—— was finished
the family did not like it. My mother withdrew the canvas
and painted another picture on its back, of our garden door,
seen from outside in full sunlight. The other day, when I
was going over old pictures, I came on Mrs. W——, look-

ing at me after thirty years. There she was, pale and wishy-washy, on the back side of a painting of a brilliant green door, a scarlet trumpet vine, and glimmering white china glimpsed within the interior.

My parents believed that a portrait should only be ordered because the client wanted that particular artist's view. The client presumably admired the artist's other work; in commissioning a portrait, he was in effect paying to see himself, his wife, or his children through those eyes. Yet clients were forever making their preposterous demands, not only about the mouth or the dress but about how a sitter was to be posed and what he was to be doing.

A rich, fashionable, and nice Mrs. B—— ordered a portrait of her four-year-old son. Children that young generally proved difficult to keep still, but Mrs. B—— took the time to come with the boy herself and read to him during sittings. Reading aloud was an essential in painting children, but was too often performed by some nurse who read tonelessly, and bored the child, which led to wriggling and squirming. Mrs. B——'s voice was low, an excellent thing in woman; her choice of reading matter just absorbing enough. The portrait of the fat little tow-haired boy, wearing blue overalls and holding a red zinnia he had snatched out of a vase the first morning, showed every promising sign for four or five sittings. Mrs. B—— loved it. Then, one day, she brought her husband to see it.

"He hated it and he hated me," my mother reported to my father that night. "He slammed around this room, scowling and objecting to everything. What am I going to *do?*"

"Ignore him," my father advised.

"I can ignore his saying it doesn't look like his child. And I can endure his showing he didn't think it was any good," she said, though doubtfully. "But he says he won't have any son of his painted holding a flower."

"Oh, for God's sake!" my father said.

In the end, my mother took the flower out and painted the little boy with his hands clasped across his middle. Mr. B—— accepted the portrait, though still scowling and objecting and refraining from one complimentary word. Years later, when I was grown up, I heard through friends of Mr. B——'s, who knew nothing of the history of the painting, that the old man, now a widower, loved the portrait of his son so dearly that he kept it in the Beacon Street library that was his favorite room, and moved it to his Nahant library every summer.

While people who paid for portraits by my mother might get their own way about what they wore in them, I, who had been since infancy the built-in, free artist's model around that house, never had any such say. My mother had drawn me at the age of six weeks in my bassinet; propped up against pillows, at the age of six months, on a background of patterned roses. At the age of one, seated in a baby carriage, I made a spot in an Impressionist painting by my father. There is a portrait of me at six wearing a dark-blue straw hat with red cherries, but that is the only article of apparel in any picture of me I remember having any fondness for, and even in that portrait I look glum. At seven I was posed with my hair parted in the middle and tied with two bows, too tight, which hurt. A prize-winning painting of my mother's called "Nancy and the Map of Europe" shows me and my large doll, dressed in identical blue cotton-crêpe dresses, with waistlines up under the armpits, and white guimpes. I hated dresses with high waistlines, because the other girls wore dresses with low waistlines. For that matter, I hated my doll, too. I had to pose so much in my childhood that when I reached the age of about thirteen I finally figured out a requirement of my own. I wouldn't pose, I said, unless I could be painted with a book. So all subsequent pictures show me in the act of reading. Several are silhouetted against a window; some show the book, some don't; but all have the eyes downcast.

It was a day of knee-length skirts and hip-length waists, slave necklaces and cloche hats. My parents thought the fashions utterly hideous. (I suppose they would think the same today.) They were right, of course. They seem always to have been right when it was a matter of how things looked. A Miss H—— was painted by my mother as a débutante in a silver lace dress with a flame-colored rose on one hip. The dress ended just above the knee. My mother pled with the girl's mother to allow her to let the dress down or else cut the picture off above the edge of the dress — anything to avoid painting those two, separate knees. But the H——s were in the full swing of fashionable taste and brushed her pleas aside. They were delighted with the portrait when my mother finished it — knees and all. Years went by. So much later it seemed almost another life, my mother ran into an aged, sweet-faced Mrs. H—— at a tea. She pressed my mother's hand in hers and said, "I have a little idea! Would you — could you — touch up Carolyn's portrait? I don't know if it is possible to add a little something, just to cover the knees? I wonder if you can visualize what I mean. . . ."

"Can I visualize what she means!" my mother snorted to me. My father was dead by that time. "*Can* I visualize!"

She did paint in some silver lace over those knees, which had, Mrs. H—— confessed, caused the picture to be relegated to the attic. It had to be a piece of real silver lace, though. Mrs. H—— had to find such a piece, and it had to be tacked onto a silvery-gray dress for a live model to wear. My mother and father had the utmost contempt for painters who painted things out of their heads. Not that they wanted to paint what is sometimes called photographically; far from it. They wanted to "render the object"— an immensely subtle process involving the interplay of the painter's subjective view with the way the light actually fell upon the object. The conflict — rather, the marriage — of objectivity and subjectivity was what made art such a wildly exciting and magical thing to my parents that they cared about literally nothing else, except maybe me. To have made up a piece of silver lace out of her head would, in my mother's view, have been unintelligent, boring, and by her standards ultimately impossible. How could she possibly know, unless she saw, just how the light would make it look?

As an art student for some fifteen years in Paris, my father spent a good deal of time at Giverny, close to Monet, and was influenced by Impressionist theories. What seemed important to him and, through him, to my mother about Monet's haystacks, cathedrals, and water lilies was that, painted at a different time of day and hence in a different light, each picture was in effect a totally different subject from the others in the same series. Objects existed as seen in the light of the moment. Half an hour later, in another light, they became quite other objects.

In his class in life drawing at the Museum School, moreover, my father taught his students to render the nude in strict light and shade. Some pupils seemed never to be able to learn to find the edge of the shadow, on one side of which all was visible and to be shown, on the other side of which all was considered invisible. I took that class, when I was eighteen. I can see my father now, standing under the stark atelier skylight in his rumpled old gray suit, backing up from some student's smudgy charcoal drawing and coming up to it again, making gestures with his thumb (he never touched a pupil's drawing) and wearing a pained expression.

"Where the light falls is the light. Where the light does *not* fall is the shadow. Chiaroscuro, the clear and the obscure. Don't go mucking your drawing up with half-lights." Half-lights were the snare that seduced the undertrained; the greatest sin was to go peering into the shadow.

When my mother looked at things (and her life was given over to looking at things; in any unfamiliar house she used to keep crying, "Look at that! Look at that!" about a chair, a picture, a china bowl of flowers, until she became embarrassed by the realization that nobody else joined her), she looked with a kind of innocent, once-born stare. I can see that now, too. She held her eyes very wide open and simply stared, as though confronted by the first day of creation.

Often she saw things quite differently from other people. Colors, for instance, appeared different to her from what they seemed to me to be. She would keep talking about a blue house on the road to Gloucester, and I couldn't imagine what she was talking about, and then one day we would be driving that road together and she would cry, "There's the blue house! Look at that!" I would look, and it would be white.

"You're so *literary*," my father and mother used to complain to me. This was in no sense a compliment but referred to the instantaneous reflex of reading into color what I figured it had to be, instead of seeing it for what — in that light — it was. I remember a dress my mother owned in the latter part of her life. She called it her black dress. Although it was a very dark dress, I couldn't help knowing that it was really navy blue. It did take peering to see that, though, and my mother never peered. She just stared, and her vision and the image met for what they were.

Then there was the portrait my mother painted of Miss R——, another Boston débutante of the late twenties, whom she posed sitting sidewise, leaning forward, arms resting on a table, head turned so that it was seen three-quarters. For once, my mother plucked up the courage to assert what the sitter was to wear. Miss R—— and her mother wanted the dress in which Miss R—— had made her début. I don't think I ever saw it, but I can imagine it — hip-girdled, knee-exposing, "snappy," as we used to say. But my mother had her way, and painted Miss R—— in a Chinese robe that a missionary in-law of ours brought back from China, of dark-blue, stiff, gauzy material encrusted with gold-embroidered dragons. Only, in the painting, it was green with silver.

The R——s viewed the finished painting with pronounced disfavor. Not only was a mere three-quarters of their daughter's face visible (and, they may have reasoned, they were paying for the whole face) but she was wearing a garment that didn't remotely resemble any clothes they admired, or, for that matter, the actual Chinese robe, either — a robe demonstrably dark blue, not green. They let it be known, politely, that they could not accept the portrait.

My mother never minded when a portrait came back on her hands, because, flooded with orders as she was in those days, she always needed something to send to the exhibitions, all over the country, to which her work was invited. Portraits in private hands were hard to borrow, for people hate lending portraits; it is as if one asked for the fireplace out of their living room.

Somewhere beyond our ken Miss R—— grew older, got married, had children, lost her husband, began acquiring grandchildren, and then, out of the blue, years later, when my mother had come to Virginia to live near me, came a letter from Miss R—— to ask whether, if the portrait was still in existence, she might see it with a view to buying it. She did see it, and bought it with enthusiasm.

It was not only the clothing of women my mother found unpaintable. Male clothing was even worse. "That awful V," she called the effect a man's collar and tie make, and she invented a way to circumvent having to paint it by getting men sitters to wear scarves. (Men sitters seem to have been more amenable than women, perhaps because the artist was so beautiful.) I can remember only one portrait of hers of a man not wearing a scarf — that of the Reverend Dr. Lyman Rutledge, whom she painted in his academic robes, which came up high enough partly to obscure "that awful V."

Little boys, back in the days of Miss R——'s youth, presented no problem, since, for best, they wore light-colored
linen suits with lace or linen collars and, for every day,
shorts, that showed their bare legs. By my mother's latter
days, however, even the smallest boys had taken to dressing
like "dreadful little men," in dark suits with shirts, ties, and
long pants—"two long black tubes" she called them.

My mother's apartment in Virginia was small, what is lo-
cally called a duplex—half of a one-story house. She had
chosen it entirely because the principal room had a view window that went up to the ceiling and let in enough light to
make it suitable for a studio. She had an ingrained prejudice
against the custom of keeping window shades at half mast.
Any window shade over which *she* had any control was instantly raised to the top. What other people call the glare
she called the light.

In the South, she discovered, people were not accustomed
to thinking in terms of her rather high prices for portraits. If
she wanted to go on getting portrait orders, she would have
to lower them. She did want to go on getting them. She never even considered the contrary. Nothing irritated her more
when she was an old lady than to have someone say, "Do you
still paint?" She reduced her prices to less than a third of her
Northern high. Even so, there were difficulties. The wife of
a multimillionaire Detroiter who had retired to Albemarle
County came up to me one day in the grocery store and, after
beating about the bush, said she had seen some of my mother's portrait drawings and would love to have her grandsons
done. How much, she ventured with hesitation to ask, did

my mother charge? I told her. (It was now less than two hundred dollars for a drawing.) "Oh," cried the Detroit lady, in her mink coat. "Oh! I'm afraid I couldn't possibly afford that!" And she hurried away to the meat counter.

The Southern ladies, too, experienced great mortification in bringing themselves to speak of money to so beautiful and elegant a person as my mother. They came to me to ask her portrait prices in a sort of agony. "I just *couldn't* ask her how much she *charges*," said the mother of two sons who were later done by my mother with vast success. "She's such a *lady*."

My mother felt no such qualms. "Good heavens! Does she think I do it for nothing?" she'd say. "You'd think I was some damned amateur."

My mother never swore, normally; but to my father amateurs were always "damned amateurs," and my father's locutions lived on in my mother's vocabulary. His principles, too, remained forever hers. Once when some sitter's hard-luck story had tempted her to present him with his portrait (it is amazing the impoverishment people who think nothing of new Buicks feel when it comes to portraits), she ended by stiffening and saying, "No. Your father used to say, 'Never give away your work. People don't value what they don't have to pay for.'"

The portraits she did in Virginia were much admired, and contented clients went out of their way to bring prospective sitters to her. One such client telephoned to ask if she might bring a Mrs. W—— to tea on Thursday to see examples of my mother's work. My mother spent the intervening days hanging additional pictures, which had

been out in her little storeroom, on the walls. When four
o'clock Thursday came, the two women arrived. They drank
tea, chattered volubly, stayed for an hour or so, and then
made their departure. At the door my mother's client said,
"I'm *so* sorry you weren't able to find some pictures for us
to look at."

"I was so stunned I couldn't think of one word to say,"
my mother told me next day. "I just stood there gaping,
with this whole place plastered with my work in back of
me. What did they think I was going to do — push them in
their faces?"

She could never get used to the idea that most people
don't use their eyes except to keep from running into things.
She never learned not to feel wounded when, for example,
she'd made some charming arrangement of flowers for the
table, or placed a yellow chair in a telling position against a
rose toile curtain, and not one person at the party for which
the effect had been planned made any comment. "Nobody
liked it!" she'd wail. I had to keep persuading her that other
people didn't see what she saw. "You mean they didn't *see*
it? But it was right in front of them," she'd cry with an incredulity undiminished over the years.

I and my friends were really hardly any better, being writers and fairly sightless too. Once, at our seashore place,
after a number of literary people had passed through for a
longer or shorter time, all with eyes downcast to the glacial
boulders underfoot or the murmurous water below, while
they talked and talked of their own and other writers' work,
my mother exploded.

"Here they've come to what is *probably* the most beautiful
view on the eastern seaboard," she said, "and they don't

look at one thing! They might just as well stay in New York."

If art as she understood it alienated her from the sightless all her life, during her last years it alienated her from modern painters as well. They, too, gazed at the ground, painted by electric light, peered into the shadow — all of which was against her artistic religion. Years before, my father had been fond of declaring that modernists — meaning painters since Cézanne — were in effect saying, "Let me look into the interior of my belly."

That attitude in modern painting was what profoundly distressed her. It was not at all that modern pictures were abstractions. "Every good painting is basically an abstraction," my father used to say. Or that they were not representational. Her dismay was different from the layman's dismay. What depressed her was the loss of that rapturous meeting between the artist's private vision and the shimmering world of objects. To her it amounted to a loss of soul.

Although there always remained a demand for my mother's portraits — "When a woman wants a portrait of her children, she wants it to look like them," she would comment grimly — her work went out of style within her own lifetime. No longer was she invited to show at all the big exhibitions over the country. She did still show at some, and she did still win an occasional prize; but she, who had once sold every picture out of her exhibitions before they officially opened, now experienced that pendulum swing of fashion which, in the art of painting, is perhaps more extreme than in any other.

She had only contempt for painters of her own generation

who, cannily trimming their sails to the prevailing winds, turned out Abstract Expressionism. She couldn't believe they were being honest. She couldn't believe that anyone who had ever got into intimate artistic relation with the natural world could be satisfied by communion with self alone. Half of reality had been abandoned, it seemed to her; the inner half remained, alone and impotent. If it was against her religion to go peering into the shadow, it was even more against it to avert the eyes from that world upon which the light falls.

The year my mother died, at eighty-three, we went to Italy to see the pictures. She had seen the British and French paintings years before, but never the Italian. Among exclaiming sightseers looking up at the blackened Tintorettos that line the dim walls and ceilings of the Scuola San Rocco in Venice, my mother merely stared at the pictures for a bit and said, "I can't see anything at all."

"But look!" the friend traveling with us cried. "Just look — hard — at the wonderful drapery in that one above!"

"I can't see a thing," my mother repeated. Where the light fell was the light. Where the light did not fall was the shadow. Chiaroscuro — the clear and the obscure.

She loved looking at such paintings as had been provided with spotlights, in various galleries and churches, and she loved looking at everything in the Uffizi, where the light falls white and strong. Most of everything in Italy she loved the radiant Tuscan landscape. As she stared at the undulating olive groves we drove through, the walled towns, the castle-topped hills, I could see by her engrossed look that the special marriage of subject and object was occurring for her.

We sailed home from Genoa on an American liner. It was making the last leg of a Mediterranean cruise, and we shared a table with a retired admiral and his wife — affable people of the world. My mother and the admiral's wife, who was called something like Mrs. Haughton, seemed made to get on with each other, as two antique, elegant, and still beautiful women. Mrs. Haughton plied my mother with questions — about her genealogy, receiving answers most gratifying to her; about the problem of becoming dress for the elderly; about mutual acquaintances, of which they discovered several. Most of these were ex-sitters of my mother's — a relationship Mrs. Haughton found it slightly difficult to grasp. "Oh, you're *artistic!*" she finally exclaimed, her face clearing. My mother winced.

One day the Haughtons turned up for lunch, full of a party they had just been to in the captain's quarters. It had been a cocoa party, they reported, making a good story of it. The captain, it appeared, was a teetotaler. At noon Mrs. Haughton, as the oldest lady present, had been given the honor of pulling the cord that blew the ship's whistle. You could see what a kick the pretty old lady got out of it. "When you heard that great WHOOOO, that was me!" she said.

I took it for granted the Haughtons rated their invitation to the bridge as old Navy people. But next day we, too, found an engraved card slipped under our stateroom door inviting us to the captain's quarters at half after eleven. The captain turned out to be a handsome man of some sixty years, who told me that in his seafaring youth he had been so terrified by a tidal wave off Madeira that he never touched liquor again. The guests were handed cards printed with a recipe for the cocoa we were drinking, which was excellent. As noon approached, the captain asked my mother, delicately, if she thought perhaps she was the senior lady present.

"Yes indeed; I'm a great-grandmother," she replied.

"That beats all the grandmothers here!" the captain declared, and invited her to blow the ship's whistle at twelve.

The time came, and we all — some eight or ten of us — trooped out onto a little deck off the chartroom, where a sharp breeze was blowing. In the brilliant sunshine the ocean all around us was ruffled into peaks.

The moment came; my mother pulled the cord; and the great, deep, thrilling whistle sounded. Then we went inside. Everyone congratulated my mother on being the oldest lady present, on being a great-grandmother, on blowing the whistle.

At lunch the admiral's lady leaned across the table, her eyes sparkling. "I hear it was you who blew the whistle today!" she said. "*How* exciting!"

After lunch, when we had gone to our stateroom for a nap, my mother said, "What's so wonderful about blowing a whistle? Here I've given my whole life to painting and nobody on board says one single word about my work. All they notice is that I'm the oldest woman alive, for pity's sake."

I started to tell her no one on board would ever have heard of her work; but I couldn't.

"Did you see, though," my mother continued, "the way the ocean looked, when we went out, with the sun on it? Bright, transparent green."

"I'd call it blue," I had to say.

"You would," she said. Affectionately.

My Mother's Solitudes

I NEVER knew which came first in my mother: whether it was that being alone all day in our house in Dedham made her come to treasure solitude, or whether what I certainly grew up assuming was innate love of solitude made her choose to stay alone. Only since I grew up did it occur to me that she might have liked to see more people.

My father saw plenty of people. In the course of his two days a week teaching at the Boston Museum School, his other days crowded with models and pupils in his Boston studio, and, for much of my childhood, his weekly trip by train to Philadelphia to teach at the Pennsylvania Academy, he had reason enough to long for solitude. Groans and cries of agony arose from him when, at rare intervals, it was nec-

essary to give a dinner party. He liked to spend the early evenings before the fire with my mother and, after she had
gone to bed, sitting in his study in a barrel chair with a swinging side arm, drawing under a blue bulb shaded by a paper-
clipped sheet of paper. He would be copying the drawings
of Ingres, Watteau, and Michelangelo, the way a pianist perpetually practices; making drypoints on a copper plate with
a ruby pen; drawing some more just for the pleasure of drawing some more, until two or even three in the morning, although he had to get up at six to have his cold bath and his
breakfast before walking a mile to the station to catch the
eight-five to town.

No one, not even old friends, suspected how passionately
my parents clung to being alone. I was privy to their guilty
secret because I used to hear those groans that prefaced a
party, and I used to see their expressions of horror when the
telephone or doorbell rang. In the case of my father, it was
hard for anyone to guess he was a solitude-lover, because he
was such a witty conversationalist. His gaiety of manner
was, however, actually a shell left over from an earlier part
of his life. Among the four of his brothers who lived to
grow up, his younger brother Robbie was his favorite. Happy, outgoing, sociable, Robbie's temperament was the very
opposite of my father's. My father had been a sad little boy.
A photograph of him in about 1870, as a child of five, wearing a short tartan dress and high button boots, reveals a deeply melancholy expression. I remember his telling me that as
a young man he went through tortures when he had to appear in company, because he feared he could find absolutely
nothing whatever to say to anyone. But then, in his twen-

ties, he began going about to parties with Robbie and Robbie's host of friends. Even today, seventy years later, there are, still living, Bostonians who remember the golden Robbie. In that aura my father developed confidence, and a brand of wit — often cynical, sometimes acerbic — that was, I think, a kind of protection, and certainly belied his tender heart. Thus equipped, in the years before his marriage, he went out a good deal in Boston society.

Then Robbie took a summer walking trip in the White Mountains with a Harvard classmate. When they got thirsty, they drank from a country spring — the classmate sparingly, Robbie deep. Both came down with typhoid fever, but only the classmate survived. The gifted Robbie, some of whose poetry had already been published — the beloved, the unforgettable — was dead at twenty-five. The friends my father had made during the short sociable years he kept, but he saw them rarely, for he simply did not want to see people any more. My mother told me he told her it made him feel sick to go into society with Robbie dead. Whatever he felt he so concealed that all my life people have said to me, "Your father had such a social gift . . . so witty . . . such a conversationalist." To me, the gloomy little face in the early photograph seems a truer portrait. Before the fire, after dinner in our house in the country, he loved to read poetry aloud to my mother, but at some lines his voice would break:

> To sail beyond the sunset, and the baths
> Of all the western stars, until I die.
> It may be that the gulfs will wash us down;
> It may be we shall touch the Happy Isles
> And see the great Achilles, whom we knew. . . .

In the case of my mother, people could never believe that someone so beautiful and elegant, someone so eminently designed by nature to be stared at, should not welcome the opportunity to suffer herself to be admired. She looked like a du Maurier lady, like a duchess. I remember my father's telling me how on a trip to England during their honeymoon, when they hired a carriage and drove through Hyde Park, a disconcerting number of pedestrians took off their hats and bowed, and it finally dawned on him that they thought my mother was some great lady—titled, powerful. She had large, limpid gray eyes, a Roman nose, an exquisitely massive chin. My father said that at a dinner party during the honeymoon some gentleman declaimed, "A Napoleonic nose and a Wellingtonian chin, and a man might well meet his Waterloo, between!" My mother, who was married at barely twenty, was, I feel sure, perfectly appalled.

She was more than modest about her beauty; she was maddening. When I was myself a young girl growing up, I could not but feel it unfair when I, the type of girl to whom people said, "When you smile your face becomes quite lovely," had to listen to that raving, tearing Juno bemoan her looks. God knows what she was comparing herself with—Gainsborough's Mrs. Elliott, Mrs. Siddons as the Tragic Muse? It seemed unfair that she, alone of humanity, didn't believe she was beautiful. After a while, when she got a compliment, she learned to receive it, with surprise and pleasure. But the next compliment seemed just as astonishing to her.

When I was a little girl, I used to get into bed between my father and mother in the early mornings, when my mother was not yet really awake. My father would improve the

shining hour by telling me stories — tall tales, as all his stories were. "Did you know Mamma saved the United States
from destruction by the Germans?" he would whisper. (The
year would have been about 1916.) "The Kaiser sent his
fleet over here to take the country by storm, but spies got
wind of the plot. Suddenly President Wilson had a wonderful idea. 'Send for old Lily!' he said. So-o-o, they got
Mamma, and launched her out into New York Harbor,
swimming. And she, alone and unaided, sank the German
battleships by ramming them with her chin." At that age, I
found this story as probable as any other, and years later my
mother told me that lying there half asleep, waiting for
breakfast to be brought to her, she would wonder, vaguely,
if perhaps she hadn't sunk some battleships with her chin,
somewhere . . . just a few.

She had always been a dreamy girl. Photographs taken of
her in the year before her marriage show her sitting on the
lawn of the house in Hartford where she grew up, wearing
a long, full-skirted dress with leg-of-mutton sleeves and a
jabot. In a few of the pictures, she is leaning over the drawing she is at work on, her white face — almost Italian against
her dark hair — intent and abstracted. In another, someone
has called to her and she looks up, startled; about her that
air of hauteur everyone always noticed, and which was so
misleading. In another picture she is leaning back, hands
limp in lap, eyes downcast, as though listening to voices
from some private world.

Her private world was not at any age the same as other
girls'. At eighteen it was not the dream of beaux and dances
that, for example, her older sister's was. That sister, my

Aunt Nancy, used to tell a story to demonstrate my mother's scorn of boys. Both sisters used often to be invited to cotillions at Trinity College and to proms at Yale, and at one of the latter my mother, ravishingly beautiful, escaped a group of admirers to cling to her popular sister and hiss, "Those men want to *dance* with me! Make them *stop!*"

She thought boys were what she later learned from my father to call "the least of God's mercies." She met my father in Boston, where she went to study art. He was seventeen years older than she, a painter with fifteen years of training in the Paris ateliers, and phenomenally learned in art and art history. He was the only man who ever attracted her; for what she had been dreaming of, even when she was a little girl, was art. Art was to her so important that beside it clothes, parties, flirtations, even the idea of marriage, were trivial. When I myself began going to dances, in Boston, my mother used to view my enthusiasm with a sort of incredulity. She shocked me once when I was about eighteen by saying of one of my friends, "All she seems to want to do is get married and have children. It isn't *serious!*"

During my childhood, I would have breakfast with my father at the round dining-room table. He taught me a game to play with my bowl of Ralston or oatmeal: "Once there was an *is*land. And then one day it began to *rai-ain*. White rain. And it rained, and it rained. And then it began to *sno-ow*. And it snowed and it snowed. . . ." He and I used to duel with our knives within the depths of the jam crock — the five-pound stone jar S. S. Pierce sold strawberry jam in — to secure for ourselves the largest nuggets. It was a cheerful meal, and afterward we would walk down to the village.

My mother was, for all those years, left at home in the two-hundred-year-old cottage backing up against the woods, to pursue her secret life all day alone.

My father almost never took a day off from his work. He did not stop for any holidays, except the engrossing rituals of Christmas; he did not stop for sickness (he once discovered from an old friend, my mother's physician, who, happening to call in the evening, insisted on looking at his chest, that he was recuperating from pneumonia); he especially did not stop for Sundays, when all the pupils and models were out from underfoot and he could have his studio to himself. Thus, I don't think my father ever had the opportunity to witness one of my mother's days at home. But I did, when I had a cold and was kept out of school.

For a little girl there is no feeling of grandeur quite like being able to do as one's mother does. Now, only agreeably ailing, I, too, could have breakfast in bed, in the guest room, where I slept when I was sick, be waved goodbye to from my bedroom door by my father, and hear the loud, cheerful sounds of his departure. I was not quite grown-up lady enough, however, to resist springing from bed then, to knock on the windowpane and see my father — stout, mustachioed, bowler-hatted, equipped with galoshes and umbrella — turn on the front walk to wave up at me.

After my mother dressed, and before she went to work, she would supply me for the morning with my school assignments that would have been delivered the afternoon before by one of my classmates; also with something more solid to get my teeth into, like *Pride and Prejudice* or *Jane Eyre*. After she had straightened my bedclothes, shaken up my pillows, seen that I had a glass and pitcher of water beside my bed ("You must drink *quantities* of water, darling"), she would depart, with a sound of tapping heels, and I would plunge into the ardors of Mr. Rochester and his mad wife.

Then, gradually and by imperceptible degrees, consciousness would descend upon me — or perhaps it was that I would begin to support the consciousness — of silence. My book slipped back among the litter of other books upon the counterpane, and I would lie there and listen to the stillness and to those tiny sounds that accented the stillness. The house itself made minute, mysterious sounds — the drop of the merest splinter upon the attic floor overhead; a sigh in the walls where some old joist had further settled; the little, complaining creaks a flight of stairs makes, as though recovering from being climbed up.

I think of those days as being always in the wintertime, and perhaps they were, because that was when I caught cold. In those New England winters, snow generally covered the ground from December to March. To the right of where I lay in bed were two small-paned windows, and through them, when there was a blizzard, I saw the snow falling, falling, in a curious, leaden light. If it was a sunny day, the dazzle from the glassy crust shone through the windows excitingly, speaking of imaginary sleighs and skating parties. In the long hours of stillness I could hear the sound even the smallest leaf made as it skittered, scratching, across the crust of the snow.

From far away in the back of the house came faint domestic sounds — the coal range being shaken down, the black iron door to the oven opened and shut. I have no recollections of the hum of a vacuum cleaner, because we never owned a vacuum cleaner. Somehow things got done about the house, but not by my mother. Her mornings were, properly, for work. The sounds of her working made a principal part of that tiny accenting to the snowy silence, and I could identify each sound.

There was the sharp, steady sawing of charcoal (sharpened to a needle point with a razor blade) up and down against the sheet of Strathmore board on my mother's easel as she worked on a snow scene from the windows of the front hall that, with the aid of a wardrobe and a chest of drawers, my father used as a dressing room. There would come a pause in the sawing, and a faint rattle, while she rummaged around in the blue-edged box that French charcoal came in. A clack — she had dropped something on the floor. If it was charcoal, it fell with a small explosion. Then a scratchy, rubbing sound, which was the careful filing of the sides of her stick of charcoal against the board covered with fine sandpaper which had a handle to keep one's fingers clean. A pause. Then would recommence the sawing of the point drawn rhythmically up and down. I would go back to Miss Brontë, or make a stab at arithmetic, but every now and then I would give myself over again to rest in the long morning's stillness.

Sometime near noon, the day's letters would come pouring in through the slot in the front door, onto the hall floor, with a splash. Springing out of bed, I would run downstairs, in my warm wrapper and pink felt Daniel Green slippers with silk pompons on the toes, to pick them up. Usually there was nothing for me; still, it did no harm to look. Then I would carry the letters up to the front hall.

"Put them down there, will you, darling?" my mother would say, abstractedly. She sat, beautifully erect, on a high stool, her right arm out at full length, holding the charcoal in its French brass holder. The charcoal would be moving slowly, tentatively, as though groping, along the page, as her face kept turning, alertly, from drawing to scene outside the windows; or the charcoal would all at once move decisively, in a long line that ran down the paper — nervous, elegant, intensely black. If I stood watching for very long, my mother would drop the outstretched arm to her side and turn around as though someone had waked her up from sleep. "Gracious, go back to bed!" she would cry. "You'll catch more cold if you don't keep warm."

After lunch, which she had in the dining room, I in bed, the light would have changed too much for her to continue with the same drawing. Perhaps she would work on another drawing, of another subject, in another light, but generally she was tired out and, after writing a few letters at the secretary in her downstairs studio, would come up to her room to lie down.

I wonder what in social history happened to the institution of lying down. All ladies lay down, in my childhood, and those of my grandmother's generation lay down even longer than my mother did. My mother lay down, flat on her back, without reading — to rest her eyes — for an hour, for two hours. The basalt clock downstairs in my father's study was abruptly audible to me, ticking. Then it vanished out of hearing again. The light changed, faded, became more leaden. It would snow again by night. Across the upstairs hall I could hear my mother sigh as she turned her cheek on her pillow. Outdoors, something — a twig, a privet berry — dropped off a tree onto the crust of the snow with a sharp if minute report. The bed I lay in, made of wood the color of maple sugar, creaked in headboard and footboard as I turned over, and *Kidnapped* and my Latin grammar slid off onto the floor.

Four o'clock came, and with it the most unlikely possibility that somebody would come to call. The time of day required that my mother be up and dressed, but because of the cold and because of the snow and because of my mother's obvious disinclination to society, the chances were that we would be left alone for the rest of the waning day, until at last, after dark had completely fallen, slammings and crashings and shouts would announce the homecoming of my father, bearing such tidings as that the temperature at the railroad station had reached ten below.

It was, I suppose, understandable enough that I as a young girl often felt myself abused because my parents were not supplying me with the sort of busy, animated, sociable household, full of comings and goings and community get-togethers, that I read about in the women's magazines on the long golden-oak table at the public library. Reforms one is helpless to accomplish in adolescence often develop, however, into the crusading instinct later in life, when one's parents are relatively at one's mercy. By the time I was middle-aged I had, alas, only my mother left to reform. I had decided in recent years that it was partly my father's recoil from society that had been the cause of my mother's lonely way of life, and I determined that she should now, at least, lead a more normal existence. The way I analyzed it, marrying an embittered older man when she was hardly more than a child had left her no opportunity to develop relationships with those of her own age. Those of her own age by this time meant people in the sixties or over. I felt it important she see a lot of them. After I moved from New York to Virginia, I persuaded my mother to give up the house in Dedham, which was by now a young-married suburb, and move to an apartment near where I lived.

Sure enough. In the ambience of all those warmhearted and company-loving Southerners, my mother opened like a flower. She went to more parties in a month than she had gone to in five years, back in New England. She was wildly popular at parties. I can see her now, standing in the middle of an admiring, chattering group, looking wonderful in a broad-brimmed black velvet hat, wearing one of her chokers with a bow, also in black velvet, cunningly designed by her to conceal any folds in her neck — tall, silver-haired, beautifully erect. The Virginians were ecstatic over her looks and her gentle manner — "She's the best thing that's happened to Charlottesville in ten years," one lady declared — and my mother in turn sparkled in the light of this admiration. She talked, she laughed, she responded. In that big hat, cheeks flushed, she looked like a successful débutante.

Although she could by this time allow herself to enjoy a whirl, I can see that none of it really changed her much. To the day of her death she groaned when the telephone or the doorbell rang. Once when my Aunt Nancy was visiting and she and I were sitting out on the terrace together, my mother came out to where we were and said in low, sibilant tones, "The B——s have come, and all they want to do is *talk*."

Her horror of society came out most strongly, of course, in relation to her painting, which she continued to do until she died. One of the remarkable things about her was that in certain branches of her work she became greater, not lesser, with age. In her early eighties my mother produced some of her best portrait drawings, working, as ever, with arm outstretched at full length without a tremor for four hours, although by that time she could not hold a cup and saucer without rattling it.

I thought, in my zeal for her welfare, that it would be nice for her also to take part in some community doings of a less frivolous nature, and to that end urged her to join the League of Women Voters. Obedient as a little girl, good as gold, she joined. One day in winter I went to see her and found her lying down, at three o'clock in the afternoon, as of yore.

"You aren't really tired. Now, are you?" I asked. "How about a little walk?"

"I've been painting all morning and I'm exhausted," she said firmly. "Eugene Speicher used to go to *bed* for the rest of the day, when *he'd* had a portrait sitting."

"I'd hoped you could fit in the League luncheon meeting this noon," I said. "I've just come from there."

My mother regarded me with large, gray, young eyes. "I went to a couple of those meetings," she said. "All they want to do is talk about politics. They're not *serious*."

We sat together then for a while before she got up to

make tea, in one of those long silences when tiny sounds become brilliantly distinct — the occasional *clunk* of the electric clock on the wall of the kitchenette in that small, peaceful apartment; the creak, as my great-grandfather's sea chest in the parlor settled a bit; the sound of a chunk of wet snow as it slid off the roof onto more wet snow; the sound of a car passing outside, coming to us muffled, as though from far away.

I have felt a sense of silence like that in one other place — in a big church to which I did not even belong. It was during Communion, and there was a hush that was merely accentuated by the sound of the priest's voice murmuring over and over, "The Blood of our Lord Jesus Christ, which was shed for thee . . ." The communicants filed up in silence; those who had returned knelt silent in their pews. The vast structure was as still as death; even when the Gloria was sung it came only as the quietest awakening —"Lamb of God . . . that takest away the sins of the world . . ."

Since in the church I was surrounded by hundreds of people, I must suppose that the similarity of those silences has more to do with me than with my mother, for her reactions to going to church were anything but restful. She once said at the church door after service, to the minister of the Unitarian church to which, out of sentiment for my father's family tradition, she used to go, "I'd come to church oftener, but it always makes me feel completely exhausted."

I saw the old man look into her earnest, forever-young face for a moment, before he said gently, "It's supposed to make you feel just the opposite."

It dawns on me that the silences I knew with my mother

came to me not from being alone at all but from being close to her. They may have emanated out of her solitude, but for her being alone did not mean silence. She was listening, calmly rapt, to that humming dynamo, her secret source.

The Girl with the Goat-Cart

THE first time I saw her she was driving a red goat-cart hitched to a real white goat. We had come to Dedham to look at the house we soon after moved into, and were driving away in a hired surrey. It was at the back of Federal Hill, where the road turns before descending, that we passed the little girl with bright yellow hair, driving her goat-cart on the side of the road. Some of the excitement I felt about moving into a new house came from knowing that there were things like goat-carts, and girls that drove them, on Federal Hill.

Her name was Kitty Bailey. She lived with her father, a real-estate man, and her mother and brother, in the last house on the hill, a house with a screened front porch with a hammock on it. They used to sit out on the porch in the late afternoon in the summer, and through the shrubbery, through the vines that climbed the screening, I could see their white clothes and hear the brother, Morton, playing on his mandolin.

It took quite a time before I got to know any of the people on the hill. They had to get used to artists; they had to get used to seeing me pass in the road. I played with the only child my age, a little boy who lived across the street, but the rest of the children, like Kitty Bailey, were too old to need me, and so months passed while I wandered past the houses on the hill, until we all got used to each other.

Mr. Bailey was a big stout man with two blue chins and very black thick hair. In the hot summer weather his striped shirt stuck to his stomach as he climbed the hill on the way home from work, and he held his stiff straw hat in his hand. Mrs. Bailey was small and thin and sandy, with pince-nez nipping the loose skin on top of her sharp nose. Morton was about sixteen; he swung his shoulders from side to side as he walked down the hill to high school.

But Kitty was always the thrilling one to me on account of the goat-cart, although I cannot remember ever having seen the goat-cart again. Perhaps it was borrowed. But I had started out thinking with fascination of Kitty Bailey and I kept on. She was at least two years older than I was and she wore very starchy skirts and swung them. Her yellow hair was tied with a big black bow on top and again in the back of the neck with another bow to match. She walked down the road with her nose in the air.

"She's a sonsy little snip," my father said. It was a favorite word of his, Scots, and meant, roughly, "cute." "Someday she'll trip and break her sweet little neck."

For a while she was much too old to bother with me, but one summer day when it was very hot and there was nothing to do and the lazy cicadas squealed down in the fields beyond the hill, I wandered up the road past the Baileys' house and Kitty was sitting on the front steps, outside the door to the screened porch. She had on a pink-and-white striped dress, full of starch.

"Hello," she said.

"Hello."

"Do you want to write in my book? I'll let you."

I opened the gate in the picket fence and went up between the shrubbery to the steps. Beside Kitty was a large flat album. I sat down on the step below her and she put the book in my lap, open at a pink page. All the pages were different colors — pink and yellow and orange and violet and green. She handed me an indelible pencil.

"You have to swear to tell the truth, the whole truth, and nothing but the truth."

In a column of questions on the left-hand side of the page, the book demanded of me my favorite color, my favorite food, favorite animal, favorite man, favorite woman, favorite time of year, and many other kinds of favorite. I loved answering these inquiries into my tastes. When I got to the bottom of the page, Kitty took the book away from me and looked.

"You didn't tell the truth, the whole truth, and nothing but the truth."

"I did so."

She pointed to where, after "Favorite Man," I had written, "My father."

"Nobody's favorite man is their *father*. I know who your favorite man is! Lester Williams! You didn't tell the whole truth!"

Lester Williams was the little boy across the street from our house. He was my age, about eight. It had never occurred to me that he was a man. But now I felt hot and embarrassed.

"I did so."

"You did not. *I* know who loves Lester! *I* know who loves Lester! Hanh-hanh!" she chanted.

But my father was my favorite man. Far and away. I told him what I had written in Kitty's book, and that she didn't believe me and had said I loved old Lester.

"Don't you care," he said. "She's too smart. Someday she's going to break her sweet little neck. You're my favorite girl, too."

That was the time of the First World War and my father was in the State Guard. He hated it, because it was so stupid and boring, but he felt it was his duty. On the nights when there was drill, he would come home from his studio with one corner of his mouth pulled down in a way that meant he was getting ready to endure something. After supper he put on his uniform. The khaki breeches were baggy and he never learned how to wind the puttees neatly. He put the khaki hat, with the felt brim and the blue cord tied with two acorns at the tips, on the top of his head, and went off with the cold night wind making his blue eyes water.

He knew how bad he was at drilling, and made fun of himself to me. "But it *hurts* an old gentleman when we have to fall flat on our bellies," he would say. My heart was torn with anguish for him — for my wonderful father undergoing pain and humiliation with those awful men. He would imitate them to me, too, and I could hear their jeering, hard voices. "Get a little pep into it!" they cried gleefully. "Make it snappy!"

Mr. Bailey was sergeant of the State Guard company. Sometimes I saw him, after supper when it was still light, stamping down the road in his uniform, with his blue chins hanging over the collar. "I suppose Bailey is a good enough fellow," my father said. "But he is a bully."

When my father got up, early in the morning, he always sang or shouted at the top of his lungs. In the mornings after drill nights, he would shout commands. "Company . . . ten . . . *shun!*" he roared. "Present . . . *arms!*" Lying in bed I could hear him stamp around while he put his clothes on. He jerked out the word "Company" in the approved military way — "*Cubady . . .*" And after a while he would get into a kind of monotonous chant, which he continued as he marched downstairs for his breakfast — "In de rear . . . *march!* In de rear . . . *march!* In de rear . . . *march!*"

I knew that Mr. Bailey was a bully and I looked at him coldly on my father's account. No wonder he was not his daughter's favorite man. And he probably had no affection for her, either. Other families than mine, I was learning, did not seem to have the same attachment to each other that we had.

Some mornings Mr. Bailey, my father, Kitty, and I would all walk down the hill to the village together, the men on their way to the train and Kitty and I going to school. The two men plugged along side by side with their hats set on their heads, and I walked beside my father, holding his hand. But Kitty did not hold her father's hand. She skipped backward down the black tar road, just ahead of us, chanting in that gloating, gleeful way, "Can't catch a flea! Can't catch a flea!" Sometimes my father pretended to make a grab for her, and she would dance out of reach and jeer, "Can't catch a flea-ea!"

Mr. Bailey just went stumping along, paying no attention to her.

"You'd better look out," my father used to say to her. "You're going to fall down and break your sweet little neck."

In those days, when the winter came it was long and iron-hard. The houses on the hill had thick soft white quilts on their roofs, until something disturbed them and the snow fell off with a noise like thunder. Sometimes after a blizzard the snow covered the tops of the picket and paling fences so that the land was flat between the houses and you could walk right over the top on snowshoes. On the worst days the carts from the stores in the village could not get up the hill, and I went downtown for supplies on my snowshoes.

In one of these winters, some time after Christmas, just after the war was over, Kitty Bailey was taken ill with influenza. I remember Dr. Perkins's sleigh standing daily outside the Baileys' gate and jingling away again down the hill. The pipes froze in most of the houses on the hill, including the Baileys', and I remember helping melt snow to take over to the Baileys' in buckets. After a while, in the cold winter, with all the snow outside, Kitty died. And very shortly afterward, in perhaps a week, Mr. Bailey died, too. Somebody said that he had sat up every night beside Kitty's bed while she was ill.

They were the first persons I had ever known to die. It was very strange. It made an impression on me when my father said, "I feel awfully bad about telling that poor little thing she was going to fall down and break her neck." I too felt full of remorse, for thinking about Kitty and her father the way I had.

Nowadays I assume, when I think about it, that Mr. Bailey caught Kitty's influenza — which was the dreadful kind of the epidemic of 1918-19 — and died of it. But for a long time after it happened I was quite sure that Mr. Bailey had died of sorrow, for his daughter.

Mrs. Harcourt's Mare

SOMETIMES — I see it as in autumn — I would be standing alone out under the pine tree in front of our Dedham house, getting over a cold, and Mrs. Harcourt would
ride by on her black mare. As she came trotting up the last
bit of hill she would call to me in her high, sweet voice,
and wave; then her horse would feel the ground leveling
out under her hoofs, Mrs. Harcourt would give a kick with
her little black boot, and they would be off — the dark-
blue skirt of her habit fluttering, the ends of her veil, tied behind the knot of yellow hair under her bowler hat, standing
straight out on the wind. I would stare after them, my fancy
galloping, too.

Mrs. Harcourt was so dashing, so free, so different from

us. For one thing, I had picked up from scraps of my parents' conversation at the dinner table that she had no business riding at all. She had some illness that made going out on a horse alone the height of unwisdom; "seizures" was the word they used. But, my mother said with a vertical line of worry between her eyebrows, Mrs. Harcourt would not put up with an accompanying groom; she would not ride in frequented places; she insisted upon having her own way. Grieved concern was in my mother's voice when she said this, but I glowed with approval.

"She won't listen to me, when I tell her how it disturbs her friends," my mother said.

"She always has to be the one to do the giving. Advice, too," my father said, a trifle sourly.

Mrs. Harcourt, the richest woman in the town where we lived, had been very kind to our family always — providing a nurse when I was little, arranging seaside vacations for my overtired mother (for it was only her own health that Mrs. Harcourt ignored), buying my father's pictures (for she was a patron of the arts). We owed her, my mother said, everything. All this made me profoundly uncomfortable when we went to Mrs. Harcourt's to tea. I felt different there from the way I felt anywhere else, I throbbed with the sense of being a representative of a humble, cautious family who owed our hostess everything.

We used to sit in the little room opening off a stair landing in that large, white house — an upstairs sitting room it was, with a tiny fire sparkling in the grate, with silver tea things on a silver tray, and a porringer with a cover that stood on the hearth, to keep warm the yellow muffins inside it. "Muffies," Mrs. Harcourt called them. Over all was an air ineffable, personal, distinguished. The smile on my face felt pasted on, like dried calamine lotion.

My mother seemed able to express quite easily the sense of deep gratitude and affection she felt for Mrs. Harcourt. She could chatter for an hour about my father's painting and her own, while Mrs. Harcourt, her hands clasped, would now and then interject, "How thrilling!" It was a favorite word of hers. Then my mother would get up, saying, "We mustn't take up any more of your time. It was so sweet and thoughtful of you to ask us; to give us such pleasure."

Mrs. Harcourt would rise, too — shorter, somewhat stocky, with curly yellow hair and a square, determined face lit by flashing eyes. "Riley will drive you home," she would say, and my mother would exclaim with appreciation. I myself could only smile — smile at Mrs. Harcourt, and at the Irish maids who came to take the tea things away, and at the dachshund who nipped at my ankles in the white-paneled hall. I had found through long experience that if I said anything at all in this house, what I said sounded forced, artificial, idiotic. "Thank you so much," I would mutter on parting, as I shook our benefactor's hand. Even that sounded false. Mrs. Harcourt would lay her hand on my stiff shoulder for an instant and go back to my mother, walking beside her out to the shining black limousine. Mrs. Harcourt never stood on ceremony; she was warm, informal, enthusiastic. My mother was warm back. It was only I who was bothered by the chasm that seemed to separate Mrs. Harcourt's great house from our small snug one, and

Mrs. Harcourt's generosity and recklessness from our own mean caution.

In the New England of my childhood, when a member of our family caught a cold it was taken seriously. The furnace, which in theory heated our house, sent what trickles of warmth did get upstairs through the register of the guest room that we called my grandmother's room, because it was hers when she stayed with us. It was in there that I was apt to be put to bed, under plenty of blankets and a down quilt. When I would lie in that square, sun-flooded room with its ceiling broken at one side by the angle of the eaves, my favorite books to read were Miss Austen, Mrs. Ewing, Stevenson, Poe; all in sets that had been presented to me by Mrs. Harcourt. I would sip lemonade, and at intervals lay my book aside to eat dropped eggs on toast, and cottage pudding with lemon sauce, off a tray that had rosebuds painted on it.

The school I went to, Miss Brewster's, *wanted* its pupils kept at home if they had colds. It did not want germs circulating in class. Homework would be brought to the ailing by some hale contemporary on her way from school in the afternoon; I would hear her voice at the front door as she left my books, and my mother's voice hustling her away again — "You mustn't catch our colds!" It was only the children that went to the public school who were allowed to go around with runny noses and sore lips, regardless; like the children in the Dreadful Hollow.

That was my father's name for it. When he and I used to walk down the hill together in the mornings, I to school, he to the train, the road, as it led past the County Meadows, was flanked with willow trees, through which a bitter wind forever whistled. We passed only one building in that stretch, Mr. Barlow's barn, and sometimes the old man would be getting his white horse out as we hurried past, with frost sparkling in his beard and in the horse's mane. Bracing himself against the winter's gale, he would hitch the horse to a blue cart with two high wheels, and drive rumbling away. We would have passed the worst of it by then, and in a minute come to where a row of mean houses on either side of the road broke the wind. We would walk slower, catching our breath. " 'I *hate* the dreadful hollow behind the little wood,' " my father would murmur, quoting from Tennyson's *Maud,* though I didn't know it.

In my childhood there were still country slums, and this was one of them. The houses were old, paintless, with rags stuffed in their windows and decaying steps. Out of the windows peered white, narrow faces; undernourished, suspicious. I did not so much hate the Dreadful Hollow as fear it. It was not so frightening in the mornings, when I could pass through it by the side of my omnipotent father, but in the afternoons, walking home alone from school, my heart sank as I descended the slope that led past the Harrigans', the Petropuccis', the Morans', the Howards'. I knew their names, everybody knew their names, for they were called in from time to time to work in more prosperous parts of town — to do a day's wash or to nail up sagging gutter pipes. On those occasions, possessions had often been known mysteriously to disappear — a whole packet of nails, a step-ladder, a half-dozen dish towels. It was a fact, I had heard my mother tell my father, that the people from the Hollow would rather steal than receive honest charity. They made it impossible, she said, for you to give them anything; medicines or clothes or comforts of any kind. They slammed the door in your face and called rude words from within. One of the men in the Hollow was said to be serving a long term in jail.

When I would be walking home from school, the Dreadful Hollow children would be playing out in their bare dirt yards, noses perpetually running, eyes red and watery. The doors of their houses stood grimly shut, but sometimes a ragged curtain would stir a trifle as I passed by. The older boys made inarticulate jeering noises at me; the girls looked at me and I back at them. Their faces seemed different from the faces of my schoolmates. They were wide and pale and blank, and had slit eyes without eyelashes. Their appearance gave me a sense of indefinable, intimate horror, as though I were somehow joined to them, as though they were partly me. I tried to keep my eyes straight ahead; tried not to care what taunts might be yelled. Sticks and stones could break my bones but words — I told myself, denying the evidence of my senses — would never hurt me. One day as I was walking home, screams rent the Hollow's air, and a tiny child, not more than six, came running around the corner of a house with her father after her — an unshaven man in shirtsleeves, brandishing a bunch of short leather straps, a device that could have no other purpose than that of flogging children.

For a long time I could not get that scene out of my mind — the father, coughing as he ran, and the terrified child with her face streaked by tears and snot. Terrible people like these were the only other people I had ever known to ignore illness.

Mrs. Harcourt's suffering, both in that illness of hers and in a certain curious sorrow, seemed to me of a high and admirable kind. Children do not so much tell themselves stories about people as they instantly convert into images what they hear said about them. It was so when my mother remarked at dinner one night, "She is such a high-spirited human being. So sensitive to the banal"—a word I recognized as one of Mrs. Harcourt's favorites. "It seems a pity," she went on, "that he can't be more on her level." When my father replied somewhat wryly, "Yes, good old Harcourt is earthy, all right," what I mentally saw, clearly, calmly, was Mrs. Harcourt standing on the landing of the great white staircase, her chin lifted very high, while up the stairs toward her groped Mr. Harcourt, whom I had seen so seldom as to leave me free to imagine him as dreadful as I liked. He was holding his hands, black with sticky earth, out in front of him, to rub them viciously upon her pure white dress. Why a man should delight in wiping his hands on his wife's clothes against her will, I could not explain to myself; but somehow the idea rang true, and carried genuine horror. Although I never felt in the least natural in Mrs. Harcourt's presence, and although her high, clear voice seemed never quite addressing me but somebody else behind or above me, nevertheless, especially when I was away from her, I knew she was a heroine and worthy of emulation. You would never find Mrs. Harcourt skulking drearily around, getting over a cold!

That was what I was doing, the afternoon I saw her ride

by on her horse for the last time. It was a day in spring, and
I was standing under the great pine that grew close to the bar-
berry hedge that edged our lawn. I heard the sound of
hoofs coming up the hill, and in a moment saw Mrs. Harcourt, riding the black mare. She sat her horse as securely as
though pinned into her sidesaddle; her shoulders in the dark-
blue habit were square and straight; her bowler was set
down neatly over her eyes. "Hello!" she called, like a silver
bell tinkling. She waved with the hand that held a crop. I
waved morosely back, conscious of all my own bondage to
mediocrity. A moment more and she had dealt a little kick
to the mare's flank. In the sudden thunder of their galloping
I watched them whirl up the dirt road that led past our
house, down a dale, and so off into the woods.

Promising myself for the hundredth time that when I
grew up and could do what I chose I, too, would ride furiously, especially if advised not to, I went back to my des-
ultory occupations: playing with some doll's furniture I had
arranged in a room that was a hole in the roots of the pine
tree; picking and chewing the young sour grass that was coming up; planting myself in the center of the circle of extra-
fine grass that grew, mysteriously, in the middle of one side
of the lawn. My mother said it was the relic of a flowerbed
of some long-gone tenant of our house, but I had decided,
years before, when I was little, that it was the manifestation
of fairy influences — a special spot, conferring special powers.

I had just willed Ellen Parsons to develop warts all over
her face when I heard the hammer of hoofs coming back
again. They were coming very fast — too fast, somehow. I
jumped to my feet. Down the road from the woods came

pounding the black mare, riderless, the empty stirrup slapping and flying wildly.

I knew I should go and tell my mother what I had just seen, but I hesitated. I had the feeling that if I did so I might be interfering with Mrs. Harcourt's intentions. Perhaps she had sent the horse home, I thought queerly. Perhaps she wanted to stay out there all alone, down in some hollow in the deepest woods, where it was dim and secret and damp, and the frogs were singing their springtime chorus. . . . I knew that I was only inventing, but I also knew that I had no conception of what Mrs. Harcourt might not be up to. She was capable of more than I was capable of imagining.

Then my years and my excitement asserted themselves, and I dashed into the house shouting, "Mother! Mother! Mrs. Harcourt's horse just went by with nobody on it!"

Moments of consciousness, in a child, are never contiguous, but occur in tiny separate explosions; so that events of those early days tend in memory to roll about like unstrung colored beads in a bowl. But there are a few memories of my childhood that do join, and the day of Mrs. Harcourt's fall from her horse in a seizure, her concussion of the brain, and the beginning of her long years of invalidism connects forever for me with the day after school got out the same year; I think it was the same year.

I was bursting with my freedom that morning in early June. As I walked up the road that led past our house, summer was just beginning to glisten and to sing. The last of the buttercups were in the fields, and the first of the silver-white daisies with their yellow hearts. Bees bumbled through the sweet air, to light upon blossoms of the trumpet vine and the syringa. I scuffed blissfully at the white stones that littered the road as I wandered along zigzagging. The road passed, after a while, between two hedges of lilac, six feet high or more, with great nodding blossoms, both purple and white. Their scent was so exquisite that I stopped short in my tracks to smell it.

As I stood there sniffing, into my state of heaven there crawled like a maggot, like a dark screen drawn across bright nature, the recollection of that day in spring, when the black horse had come galloping down the same road leaving Mrs. Harcourt insensible beside the rock her head had struck when she fell. The memory was so foreign to my mood and to the day that I could only blink. Then it drifted out of my head, and I did not think of it for years and years.

There Is a Host Approaching Nigh

THESE autumn Saturdays, usually just about when we have finished lunch, as I stand in front of the south window in the kitchen of our winter house scraping the dishes over the sink, I will hear a rapid drumbeat, and the sound of martial music is carried to me on the soft November air. It is the University of Virginia band, marching to Scott Stadium for the football game. Most of the tunes it plays are familiar to me. As I wash the plates and cups I start to sing along with them, only the words I sing are often not the same as the words they are singing to the music over there.

My husband, who is a professor, takes the reasonable attitude that since he went conscientiously to every football game Brown played when he was an undergraduate, every

game Harvard played when he was working for his doc-
torate, every game Princeton played when he started out as
a young instructor until the day it was revealed unto him
that football is a dull game that he cares nothing about, he
need never waste another Saturday afternoon.

My own ardor, as I continue to sing to the stirring, far-
away music of the band, has little to do with football as a
sport. I, too, went to every game Harvard played — during the five or six years when I was, first, a Boston sub-
débutante, then a débutante, then what used to be called
L.O.P.H. ("Left on Poppa's Hands"), yet in all that time I
never became absolutely certain what a first down was.

My feelings about football games, which are deep, go far
back into my childhood to the day when my father and my
Uncle Edward took me to see my first, a Yale-Harvard
game in the Harvard Stadium. Harvard won the game — at
the time this did not surprise me — and today I can remember all the words of all the songs we sang that cold November day; which is why I am able, after all these years,
to sing Harvard's words to the tunes the Virginia band is
playing, while over at Scott Stadium they are singing other
versions.

But I don't quite sing Harvard's words, either. The way I
begin one of the songs is "Buck the line for Harvard, For
Harvard wins today . . ." When my younger son, then a Harvard junior, overheard me at this, he exclaimed "Mother!"
in tones of the deepest outrage, embarrassment, and disgust.
"The actual words are 'Hit the line for Harvard,' in case
you are interested," he added coldly.

"I know," I said. "But I'm singing Grandpa's words."

"You couldn't be! He *couldn't* have sung that," he insisted so feverishly that I felt I had better get to the bottom of what it was he thought I was singing. There proved to have been a mistake. He thought I had sung "Butt the line for Harvard," and, familiar with my ignorance of the most elementary rules governing sports, feared that I was confusing football and soccer.

My father, a highly original man, had his own version of most things. He had managed to be the only male in several generations of his family — and among several brothers — who did not go to Harvard. After passing its entrance examinations he departed for Paris to study painting. On returning to Boston he plunged into a career entirely devoted to the practice, teaching, and criticism of art. But he was not content to rest upon these atypical laurels. Instead, he became the most ardent Harvard rooter in all his family. He went to its games, read its news, upheld its name, to an extent that the other brothers still living — an architect, a professor of English, and a railroad man — never dreamed of.

Perhaps, by going there, they had got Harvard out of their systems. My father never got Harvard out of his system. I remember, as a child, hearing him say about a boy cousin of mine whose family sent him to Yale, "That was a damned silly thing to do. Why should anybody send a son to a little place like Yale or Princeton when there *is* Harvard?"

My childhood was for some reason overlaid by a haze of melancholy. The suburban streets, deep in russet leaves I scuffed through on my way home from school; the country road behind our house (covered with white stones that at an earlier, happier stage I had believed to be dragon's teeth), up which I wandered to lonely, autumnal woods; our house and grounds, seemingly always silent, unpeopled, lifeless, filled me with sorrow and resignation. That was the way this place was, and there was nothing a child, an unpopular child, could do about it.

My days were redeemed by the appearance of my father, who generally got home from his studio in Boston about half an hour before dinner. When I was little, I used to be in bed by that time, and he would come upstairs and tell me stories of Paris, of landscape painting in Holland, and of wine tours taken on a bicycle all over France. But as I grew older, his belief that I should learn to take part in grown-up conversation made possible long hours at the round dining-room table, where I sat between my gay, witty father and my beautiful mother, and inhaled my education.

It was during such a dinner hour that my mother said, "I had a letter today from your brother Edward. He's coming to stay with us over the Harvard-Yale football game."

"Good," my father said. "He said he'd get me a ticket."

"He's got three," my mother said. "He was kind enough to suggest I come too. Do you think he'd mind awfully if I declined? All the barberries are going to drop off that branch if I don't finish my still-life."

"Art first, life afterward," my father said. "How would *you* like to go, old socks?"

All I could reply was "Oh!"

Uncle Edward — my professor uncle — was a great favorite of mine and I was a great favorite of his. During moments of demonstrativeness he would call me his chocolate cucumber, referring to a box of candy he had once brought me, impelled principally by scholarly curiosity as to what a chocolate cucumber could possibly be. (They turned out to be quite good.) He was a very tall man, so thin that he was known to his loving students as Spike, and, like many thin men, he could keep on eating almost indefinitely. My mother had once kept on asking Uncle Edward to have another piece of pumpkin pie and each time, absorbed in conversation, he had passed up his plate; the only reason she stopped asking him and he stopped eating was that a second pie ran out. He spoke in a voice so dry as to be almost flat; and this tone of his, for some reason, was deeply reassuring to me. It was as if it counteracted, nullified, the mysterious sadness that overclouded my life.

Unlike Uncle Edward, my father was given to bursts of ebullience. He always departed for his studio in a great flurry of lost outer garments and shouted farewells. This routine he followed as usual on the morning of my first football game.

"Meet you in Harvard Square at twelve!" he called to me and Uncle Edward as we continued to sit at the breakfast table, soberly partaking of Cream of Wheat. The front door slammed, and he was gone.

"I never saw a man so wedded to his art," Uncle Edward observed, helping himself to a large spoonful of strawberry jam.

"Every moment lost from the studio is a moment wasted, to him," my mother replied, half proud, half mournful. She had come down to breakfast because we had a guest. She rose hurriedly from the table to go out to the kitchen and accomplish the giving of the day's orders, so that she could get on with her still-life.

"When you have climbed out of the jam pot," Uncle Edward said to me, "we might go for a walk."

We went far up the stony road in the chill, early, echoing November morning. Uncle Edward was a member of the Appalachian Mountain Walking Club, and always able to introduce me to new secrets of woodcraft. This time, I remember, he drew a penknife from his pocket and showed me how to peel birch bark, in a wide strip, off a tree back in the leafless woods. The sun sent faint watery rays down the pine-needle paths that were first trodden, Uncle Edward had told me, hundreds of years ago by the Indians. It did not seem sad or lonely here any longer, but quiet, peaceful, and interesting.

"Time to get started," he said, looking at his gold pocket watch. My stomach contracted as I remembered the excitements ahead.

We took the train to Boston, and from there the subway to Cambridge. At every stage of our journey the crowds became denser, noisier, gayer, until we emerged into a Harvard Square swaying with raccoon coats, red velvet and blue felt cloche hats, crimson banners with an H, blue banners with a Y, enormous chrysanthemums, and bright-plaid steamer rugs carried over people's arms.

We stood waiting together on the island of the subway entrance in companionable silence, jostled as though by the waves of a cheerful, noisy ocean. In a few minutes my father appeared, waving a folded newspaper.

"Hello, old boy," he greeted his brother. "Hello, Job Lots. This is bully! Suppose we get some lunch."

I crossed the traffic jam on Massachusetts Avenue between my tall father and my taller uncle. "She shuts up like a clam whenever anything new is going on," my father reported over my head in fond, paternal tones.

"An intelligent practice," Uncle Edward replied, dryly.

We went to a place where we were supposed to put our plates of lunch on the broad single arm of our chairs. I suppose it must have been merely the Waldorf Cafeteria of those days, but to me it laid claim to a total glamour, with its laughing, pushing crowds of young men and beautiful girls. I remember the elaborate layer cake I was gravely munching when all at once the strains of martial music struck my ears.

"Come on, boys!" my father exclaimed. "We've got to see the band go over the bridge."

"Temper your transports," Uncle Edward said. "I want to finish my coffee."

When we joined the throngs in the Square, the music came to us in gusts upon the breeze. "List to the sound of the Flying Widge," sang my father with it — improvising, I realized later. "There is a band approaching nigh, Harvard is marching up the bridge. . . ."

"Deland's tactics are out of date," remarked Uncle Edward. "That yellow house is where your great-grand-uncle lived when he was president of Harvard," he added to me.

"Oh, *do* come on, Edward," my father cried. "'Behold, they come in view, Who wear the crimson hue . . .'" he continued to sing, as we turned in to Boylston Street. Before us

I could see, sure enough, with its flags waving and its band playing, Harvard marching over the Anderson Bridge.

On the way to the stadium they bought me a banner and a maroon chrysanthemum with a white H affixed to it, and a program containing the words to the songs.

"Do you think you could be a good girl and stand right here without moving, while Uncle Edward and I leave you for a minute?" my father asked when we had reached the foot of a flight of concrete steps inside the stadium.

I nodded. They moved away.

"You're sure you'll be all right?" my father called, turning around.

"She's a sensible child," Uncle Edward said, taking his arm.

Past me where I stood swept droves of the young men in their coon coats, crimson scarves, and battered gray felt hats, conducting their girls with the silken legs and high, high heels and tight little crimson skirts that came just to the knee. I stayed stock-still, obediently, in the angle of the stairs, in my school coat, pleated plaid skirt, and the red sweater I had put on specially for Harvard.

I saw my father and my uncle coming back before they saw me. They were arm in arm and deep in talk. I heard my father say, "You take just one bum steer and your whole damned life seems to go down the drain."

"You've done pretty well," Uncle Edward said. "Forget it."

A trickle of terror chilled me, and under my feet the abyss yawned. My father *not* happy?

"Good old fat sides," my father said, and took me by the

arm. We went up the stairs and emerged into the enormous, space-filled, howling, gaudy stadium.

As we found our places, facing a sign on the field that said "35," a row of young men in white sweaters with crimson H's were leading the cheering, by a series of violent physical convolutions that ended in their all turning handsprings in unison. "Har-vard . . . Har-vard . . . Har-*vard!*" the crowd roared. The cheerleaders walked up and down, clapping. The band broke forth again in brassy gaiety.

"With the Crimson in something flashing, amid the cheers of victory, Old Eli's hopes we are dashing . . ." sang my father, waving his program from side to side and sitting on the edge of the board, with seat numbers, that was under us. Surely I was mistaken about the meaning of what he had said? My anxiety turned itself around in a circle, lay down, and went to sleep. The teams ran on the field, flexing their knees.

I stood up when my father and uncle stood up, and sat down when they sat down, but I did not really understand any of the hurried explanations they kept tossing over their shoulders at me as the game progressed. Nor did I mind not understanding. The spectacle was more than sufficient. The radiantly sunny afternoon passed slowly by, as a blimp hung silently above the stadium, and now and then a small white biplane flew over. At intervals the numbers in the scoreboard at the end of the stadium disappeared with a jerk, and other numbers were jerked into their places. On the field the teams swept up, swept down, crashed head-on into total impasses, ran about in scattered disorder. Once in a while one huge-shouldered player would free himself and go running down the field alone, hugging the ball, while both sides rose to their feet like a great wave and roared. Then a player would kick the ball from the field, and it would soar up and curve over the white goalposts.

As the afternoon grew later and colder, I could see the twinkling, as of fireflies, from a thousand points of light where people on the Yale side were lighting cigarettes in the dusk. Gradually, almost imperceptibly, a moan began to rise from across the stadium. "Aaahhhhhh," it swelled, and receded again.

"That's the Undertaker Song," my father explained hastily when I pulled at his sleeve. "The Yales think they're going to win. They're not, though. We are." He returned to frantic cheering.

"Poor . . . old . . . Har . . . vard . . ." moaned the Yale side.

We did win. A player with monstrous shoulders broke loose right in front of where we sat, and ran, weaving, down past the Yale goal line. The little fat man in the middle of the field held up both arms, and in the gathering dusk the Harvard side burst out in a long, hoarse scream. Hats were thrown into the field. Uncle Edward and my father and I stood and watched the students stream down off the stands to snake-dance up the field. The goalposts tottered and went down.

Slowly we made our way down the steps and through the mobs in the field to the exit, and walked around behind the stadium to the field house. There, under a white blaze of electricity, the crowd, with upturned faces, was chanting, "We want Owen. . . . We want Owen. . . ." It was a scene of the greatest exaltation.

After a while, a young man in a heavy sort of bathrobe came to the door of the field house and waved. The crowd yelled a pitch higher, in ecstasy. I looked up into my father's face to see if he, too, was ecstatic.

But his face was sorrowful and resigned. My stricken heart sank into my stomach.

A moment later, Uncle Edward took my arm and we turned. "Well, it's been Harvard's day," Uncle Edward remarked to my father as we began to move away.

"Yep," my father said. "Some place."

Then the band, which had come up at the head of the long procession of snake-dancers, broke into a fresh tune. My father's face lighted up. "Buck the line for Harvard," he sang, waving his rolled-up program. "For Harvard wins today . . ." In the chill and violet dusk, filled with the music of the brasses, the cries of the crowds, and the strange distant echoings of twilight, we made our way back to the road, and over the bridge to the subway.

And that is the version I sing today, as I stand looking out over my backyard, washing dishes and listening to the Virginia band as it marches to Scott Stadium. I am seized by something of the old conviction that a football game is a glorious and ultimate experience that used to impel me to accept every invitation to go to the Harvard games (except one I got from a Dartmouth boy; I would not sink to sitting on the Dartmouth side). Suddenly I am tempted to let the dishes wash themselves, hurry over to the stadium, see if a ticket hasn't been turned in, go in, and watch the game.

For over there people will be waving across at friends, girls in bright-colored hats will be laughing up into their escorts' faces, banners — orange-and-blue ones — will flutter from the stands in the afternoon sunshine; the cheerleaders throw themselves about in transports; a roar rise as the team jogs onto the field and the mystic rite of football begins.

But then I have to laugh. For I can't help realizing that I would actually rather — with long delicious strokes of the brush over the dirty old white — paint the guest-room furniture Chinese red.

The Black Cape

WHEN my mother died, I inherited along with my great-grandmother's Flight-designed Royal Worcester tea set and a few preferred stocks, a fringed cape of soft black tweed that came from the once-famous Boston branch of an Edinburgh woolen concern — Romanes and Paterson. The tea set is an heirloom, the stocks an investment, but the cape is both an heirloom and an investment.

I can tell just about when my mother bought it. It had to be some time before my wedding in 1928, because a shower descended just after that ceremony and my mother threw on the cape to protect her wedding finery. What with the way I felt about clothes in those days — which was, roughly, that if one was not wearing Chanel pearls, a felt helmet and a knee-length coat held clutched together at the hip, one might as well be dead — I am sure I considered the cape beneath contempt. Capes played no part in the 1928 fashion picture. But Romanes and Paterson and my mother took a longer view.

Romanes and Paterson was, in those days, established in rooms upstairs in an office building on upper Boylston Street. The shop was held in esteem by Bostonians because the very high prices it charged were supported by superlative quality. Bostonians appreciate value. Also, Bostonian ladies, at least in those days, tended to look upon clothes as they looked upon stocks and bonds — less as adornment than as a utility to be hung on to, like principal. They took solid satisfaction in the long-lasting yard goods they could buy at Romanes and Paterson — the hound's-tooth check and bird's-eye pattern tweeds and the Glen plaid woolens, and the garments — whether ready-made or tailored to order — like Inverness capes; gored skirts that allowed of a hearty stride; stout, hairy suits; Harris tweed coats cut like their husbands'; full-length fringed capes like my mother's; and cashmere scarves, Shetland and Fair Isle sweaters, and knitted gloves. These things, displayed on shelves and tabletops, were sold without fanfare, without mention of anything so feckless as fashion, by men who spoke with a strong Scots burr, in the broad sunshine streaming in through windows that looked south over the New York, New Haven and Hartford tracks.

It was precisely this kind of Boston and this kind of attitude toward fashion that in those days I was in violent rebellion against. After I was married and went to live in New York, I instantly took a job on *Vogue,* where clothes were thought of rather differently. My boss, the late Carmel Snow, once went on record as saying that no woman should have more than three outfits in her wardrobe at a time — one on her back, one in the closet, and one at the cleaners'. This sound advice, intended to prevent women from cluttering up their closets with clothes that don't become them and that they never wear, can only be properly understood if it is realized that Mrs. Snow assumed three new outfits would be purchased at the advent of each of the four seasons. I don't know what Mrs. Snow did with her own last season's dresses, but women of fashion, generally, either gave theirs away or sold them to thrift shops or to their friends. It made headlines, in *Vogue,* when some chic lady treasured and wore a ten-year-old Mainbocher. I remember, myself, buying from Mrs. James Forrestal, for very little, two Paris suits with accompanying blouses, one evening dress, and a country suit from Vera Borea which I still have (for all my revolt against Bostonian ways, I was never wholly purged of them). I bought all the new clothes I could afford, however, and I too later gave most of them away, usually to our maid, whose name was Daisy Lonesome.

When I would go home to spend a weekend at my parents' house outside Boston, I made a great thing of being horrified at the way my mother hung on to her old clothes. My mother held a fashion philosophy — to give it the fashion-magazine name — certainly the direct opposite of *Vogue*'s. She hung on, for instance, to suits and coats from the Brookline tailor who had made the suits and coats in my trousseau. Already almost all mine were done away with, but my mother still possessed even earlier productions of his. If some coat

or suit actually got holes in it, or lost its nap, she might re-
linquish it to the Morgan Memorial — very likely first
removing a fur collar to use on something else.

My mother was very beautiful, but it seemed to me that
what clothes she did buy she bought not with a proper vanity but far too soberly. She was also given to buying clothes
I considered beyond the pale because they came from Sears
Roebuck, or Filene's basement. Bostonians are great ones
for a bargain, and in those days, in my ignorance, gener-
alizing as young people do generalize, I imagined that the
philosophy of dress my mother held was a Bostonian one.

With some haughtiness I would explain that buying new
clothes at least once a year was a necessary support to the national economy. I would look disapprovingly into her closet
and try to get her to throw out things accumulated in it. I
also tried to look disapprovingly at *her;* but I could never
quite manage it, because the irrefutable fact was that she always looked beautiful. Moreover, elegant. While most
women painters tend to dress artily, my mother wore clothes
with an air.

The sort of thing I remember recommending she throw
out included a big box full of pieces of fur — an ermine
stole with the tails attached, a chinchilla collar from an old
evening cape, a Persian lamb jacket, a sealskin muff with a
split in it; and then there was always that old black cape
with the fringe. By this time, which was about the year 1933,
I had learned a little more about my mother — enough to realize that it was impossible to get her to dispose of clothes simply because they were old. I therefore devised the sometimes
successful strategy of telling her somebody needed the garment I wanted her to get rid of.

"Poor old Mary Donovan," I remember saying, "she looked so pathetic this afternoon, all bent over and shivering when I passed her down in the Hollow. Why not give her your old black cape? You've gotten an awful lot of wear out of it."

Fired with instant sympathy, my mother agreed that this would be a splendid gift to make. But when I got back to New York I received a letter from her that mentioned she had changed her mind about the cape. "I thought a real coat would give more protection from the cold," she said. "So I gave Mary a little something, to buy what she wants at Jordan's. But it was thoughtful of you, dear, to suggest it."

Maybe it was then I got the first inkling of a suspicion that I had sized up my mother's clothes philosophy wrong. It was not entirely thriftiness, it was not at all stodginess, it was certainly not lack of taste that made my mother hang on to her clothes. She hung on to them not, actually, for Bostonian reasons, but as a sort of private expression of herself.

During the war, about the time that Romanes and Paterson — which had moved — suddenly, lamentably and forever vanished from the Boston scene, I spent a year at home with my now widowed mother, and it was then that I really got the hang of how she went about dressing herself. She collected clothes because collecting clothes allowed her to make arrangements from among them. She bought clothes whenever they appealed to her taste — not because they were expensive or because they were inexpensive, but because she decided she could use them in her arrangements. She was always a good seamstress, and made over any garment she bought to suit her fanatical standards of good fit. Her philosophy differed from that of the fashion magazines in that it was akin to that of a painter or musician, who devises a composition out of an assembled fund of motifs and themes.

My mother was so gentle she hated to criticize people, but after a while I began to realize that, far from puritanically denying herself new clothes, as I had assumed, she rather pitied the people who were so uncreative that they had to buy whatever was in the shops — whatever they got sold — and wear it just as it was. Far from having a Bostonian's indifference to style, she pitied people who were so unimaginative they could no longer see the style in a garment temporarily out of fashion. She gently pitied people so sheeplike as to be impressed by a label, and people who hadn't the taste to rearrange clothes to suit their own style — who were, for that matter, unable to develop a style of their own. All these years it had not been that she was too conservative or too economical or too Bostonian to keep buying new clothes, and keep throwing out the old ones; it was because she thought it boring — tiresome would have been her word — docilely to buy what you were told, and get rid of what you still liked.

And in some mysterious way she always looked madly fashionable. She used to make, by hand, little white muslin or organdy dickeys to wear under some black dress. She would retrim a broad-brimmed black straw hat with the exactly right, smashing, black-and-white plaid taffeta bow. She took that old, good Persian lamb jacket and had a short scarlet coat lined with it. She made black satin stocks to wear with a gray worsted suit. She often recut a new and inexpensive dress so as to give it a better line, and then wore it with an old coat that might have cost a good deal, and a sailor hat trimmed over for the third time. Sailor hats just suited her du Maurier features.

During the wartime year I spent with her, we went to one cocktail party where a lady came up to me and said, "Your mother is the most fashionably dressed woman in Boston." When we got home I told my mother and we dissolved in laughter, for everything visible she had had on that day came from Sears Roebuck, with an assist from her own needle.

"I hope you didn't enlighten her," she said. "People feel so disappointed when one's clothes don't come from Bergdorf's!"

She owned clothes that had come from Bergdorf sales, too. For she had nothing against Bergdorf's; and nothing against *Vogue*. She used to look through *Vogue* sometimes, as you would look through a cookbook, to get ideas. It was just that she felt it tiresome to spend money she didn't need to spend. She had other uses, she considered more interesting ones, for the money. She had the creative trait of never being able to leave well enough alone. Well enough was not good enough; and so she rearranged everything from clothes to houses, and would build a new wing on our granite summer house, add a new dormer to our eighteenth-century winter house, or plow out a new semicircular addition to the garden.

It was as if she didn't want to be somebody else's creation. It was also as if she didn't want to be what she herself would never have called a sucker.

As for myself, I am the result of my conditioning, so I

have gone on buying clothes and giving them away. I don't care for sewing, and I have no idea how to tailor. Although I still possess Mrs. Forrestal's Vera Borea suit, and wear it for walks in the Virginia countryside, I've disposed of almost all the clothes I bought over the forty years since I was married. I do remember some of them, and with a certain longing — a black-and-blue print dress I used to wear to the races at Belmont, and gave away to Daisy Lonesome; a beige-and-brown knitted dress with a pleated flounce at the knee; a dark blue wool surplice dress from Balenciaga, extremely becoming, that I gave away for no better reason than that it was old. Different dresses come into my memory at different times, and the reason for this is, I think, that the dresses I am remembering are the ones that would be, with a little rearrangement, right square in fashion today.

I once heard myself say, at a ladies' luncheon, "I never gave away a dress that I didn't regret it." The woman I said it to looked shocked. She thought it meant I was lacking in generosity. But what I intended to say was that in the case of my favorite dresses, there always comes a time when I would like to have them back to wear some more.

I know there is a good case to be made for keeping one's closet weeded out. A well-dressed friend of mine tells me she considers it a moral duty, for each new garment she purchases, to dispose of one she already has. But there is also a case to be made for old clothes (for women's old clothes, that is; men made their own case long ago). I would like to make a case for Mrs. Forrestal's Vera Borea suit, which is made of red, white and blue tweed that looks beige from a foot away. I would like to make a case for a coat of beige bird's-eye tweed that came from Romanes and Paterson, which is my nicest country coat and was once, though cut differently then, in my trousseau in 1928; and for my favorite tea gown, an abaya of striped yellow and black satin that my great-aunt Susan Hale brought home from Egypt when she went to visit her brother Charles, who was consul there, at the time of the opening of the Suez Canal.

I would like to make a case on the one hand against the conventional, undiscriminating discarding of clothes that still have personality and charm, and a case on the other hand in favor of my mother's Romanes and Paterson cape.

I would rather that the cape were still hers. But it is mine, now, and exactly the right length — the fringe hangs just to the hems of the black tweed suit and the black dinner dress I've so far worn it over. Its material, soft as a kitten, forms a yoke around the shoulders and buttons in front, with a long attached stole that one can tie in a rakish knot. Its extensive wear — my mother even took it to Holland in 1932 — seems not to have removed an atom of the nap from that wonderful tweed, which, the label says, was woven on the Isle of Arran.

Recently I was invited to Richmond to dine and hear the Richmond Symphony. In the interval we stood out at the entrance to the Mosque to catch a breath of air, I in my dinner dress with the cape slung over my shoulders. A woman in a mink coat, whom I hadn't seen for some time, hurried up and, after we shook hands, asked me what I'd been doing.

I said I'd just got back from New York.

"I can see that!" she said, eyeing me. "Terrific! This is

the year for capes, and fringe too, of course. You must have got *that* at Bergdorf's."

"Absolutely," I said.

Grape Jelly

NOT until I was middle-aged did I begin to suspect that perhaps my mother, by nature, had been not an artistic so much as a practical person; and that being an artist and beautiful tended to thwart her practicality. I don't know why it didn't occur to me earlier — surrounded as I was throughout my childhood by evidences of her ingenuity. Perhaps it was because in the Eden of our family standards, practical activity rather represented the snake.

Take one instance of practicality. No one could do up a package the way my mother could. She kept the wherewithal for wrapping operations out in the upstairs front hall. You passed along the side of the stair banisters, past a glass-front jelly cabinet that had been fastened to the wall by my mother herself with huge screws, to where the hall widened to contain a Victorian wardrobe, in which my father's suits hung. A door up to the attic opened off the back wall, facing two windows that gave on a view of our front lawn bordered with elms and, on the other side of the street, the seventeenth-century house that was once a posting tavern on the road to Albany.

Wrapping paper and string were kept in the drawers of a bureau opposite the wardrobe. On top of the bureau was a double row of books — one row stacked on top of the other — for which room could not be found in the living-room shelves; the not-very-good books, I suppose. I remember how once when I'd been sent to fetch wrapping materials I was trapped in one of the volumes of something called, approximately, The World Library of Great Literature, into which I'd taken a peek. I struck an episode from *She,* by Rider Haggard. Hypnotized by what I read, eyes bunging out, I raced through the account of that beautiful creature stepping into a column of fire in some subterranean cavern and instantaneously degenerating into a shriveled monkey, aeons of years old.

"What are you doing all this time?" my mother's voice demanded. Her footsteps came hurrying out to the hall. "Reading? For pity's sake!"

She bent and snatched out the paper she needed from the bureau drawer, and a hank of twine from the box of saved string. She could never truly sympathize with the seductions of reading that held my father and myself in thrall. She deeply respected the *idea* of books. I can see her, *Mont-Saint-Michel and Chartres* lying open on her lap, beside the fire in the evening. She is turning its pages, gravely. But it is the illustrations that hold her.

"Come along now," she said, turning from the string box. "It's time you learned how to tie a package."

The scene of my mother's wrapping operations was always the wide, white surface of the double bed with brown-sugar-colored posts, that my parents slept in. If the season were Christmas, her presents were tied up there — sometimes with green-and-white checked taffeta ribbon, sometimes with double-faced red satin. The tissue paper my mother used for them was not any ordinary sort, but what in our family was known as the gun paper. This was an extraordinarily tough, transparent though white-mottled, sheet my mother's father had used in the course of inventing gunsights. (In what way tissue paper fitted into that occupation none of us knew enough about guns to imagine.) In the bottom of that hall cupboard was stored a thick roll of the sheets, that diminished very, very slowly over the Christmases and birthdays of my childhood. When I was clearing out my mother's Virginia apartment I came across a thin wad: it was the last of the gun paper.

The brown wrapping paper brought from the front hall was laid on the counterpane with its written-on side up (it was, of course, used wrapping paper — wrapping paper was not a thing you bought new). Whatever was to be wrapped was laid on it with geometrical precision, the brown paper folded up and around it so that the triangles at its ends were as neat as the mitered corners of a hospital bed.

"Hold it like that while I get the twine ready," my mother said. She tied a noose in one end of the length of twine, then she slipped the other end under the package, through the noose; shifted the lines of the crossing the twine made into perfect alignment, and then adjusted the noose. I, at her word, let go of the two ends of the package, and my mother pulled. Hard. She gritted her teeth with the effort. Her Wellingtonian chin jutted.

It was on such an occasion that my father, arriving home from his studio and catching her thus, observed, "My dear, you look like a meat ax."

Her practicality was our domestic snake not only because my father naturally preferred to see her romantically beautiful, face relaxed and dreaming, hands folded loosely in her lap, eyes cast down under Italianate lids as she listened to him reading aloud by the fire after dinner. And it was not only because it annoyed him — when she was hearkening, rapt, to him discourse on art — to have her jump to her feet and go scurrying out to drive the woodchuck away from the garbage pail. Practicality had other results for my mother, as with all that cooking.

Previous to it, affairs of the kitchen had been the concern of a Bridie or Theresa or Norah who slept up in the room over the kitchen (a room with a fascination for me because of its curious smell. Its portable bathtub was made of tin painted green and shaped like an inverted broad-brimmed hat. Whoever was the current incumbent of the maid's room always seemed to keep an array of boxes on the bureau: boxes for hairpins and safety pins that were decorated with ladies in pompadours and vast, pastel hats, boxes that held writing paper in provocative shades of pink, yellow, mauve and green, and the box holding a nameless horror — resembling the stuffing in upholstered chairs — that I dimly realized was human hair).

Then, suddenly, my mother was always in the kitchen. I knew it was wartime, because we used to have something called war cake, delicious, dark, and made (it was always pointed out; there must have been some culinary triumph about it) from applesauce. I remember my mother leaning over what I recall as huge caldrons (I don't know where they came from or what became of them), a lock of her dark, wavy hair falling over her flushed forehead. She would keep batting at it, with the back of the hand that held a big wooden spoon, its bowl stained scarlet from currants or from tomatoes.

If it were currants, I watched her pour them into a cloth bag, also stained red. It made a mass that dripped all night into an enormous yellow bowl set on the floor under the shelf in the pantry from which the bag had been suspended. If it were tomatoes, I watched her put hundreds — it seemed to me — of glass jars to scald, in racks set in those same huge caldrons. Later I would watch what I gathered was an infinitely important business of transferring the steaming tomatoes into the sterilized jars and sealing the tops of the jars down with red rubber washers.

It was during this epoch that my mother also gave herself to the making of jelly from the apples in our orchard, in autumn; or, sometimes, to slicing them neatly and putting them to dry in the sun, on trays that she set in all the windowsills. Ours was an old orchard and the trees were of varieties whose fruit was even then no longer on the market — Pound Sweets, Russets, Astrakhans. We also had trees of crab apples, that made a rosier jelly. I remember my mother telling me — as I stood in the kitchen watching with my hands clasped behind my back — that the great thing about any kind of apple is that it jells better than any other fruit.

It was a piece of miscellaneous wisdom I absorbed along with all the other information drifting around our house: put the open ends of pillowcases to the outside when you make a bed (it was forty years before I figured out why); tooth powder is better for your teeth than toothpaste (I, today, get an agreeable sense of protest out of using tooth-paste); Mr. Brandeis — a lawyer who then lived in Dedham with whom my father often shared a seat on the commuting train to Boston — is more interesting than the brokers and the bankers; the best brand of paint is Winsor & Newton's.

When the apple jelly jelled, in round-bottomed jelly glass-es, I watched as my mother sealed them with a double pour-ing of paraffin, heated to smoking point in a little white enamel teapot that I used today for my breakfast coffee. Then I would help her carry them all upstairs, and put them away in the cabinet that, with her jaw set, she had screwed to the wall. Thereafter on winter afternoons I had the plea-sure of standing and viewing the rows upon rows of glasses la-beled, in my mother's beautiful and meticulous printing: Apple Jelly; Crab Apple Jelly; Currant Jelly. Grape Jelly. The year of making was always added.

We used them up at dinner with the meat course — all ex-cept the grape jelly. My father as a boy had once eaten too many grapes and the very mention of grape jelly made him shudder. My mother was too tenderhearted to bring it to the table, but she did go on making it, in enormous quantities, when grapes were in season. I had grape jelly in my school sandwiches, and my mother and I would eat it spread on bread and butter, for weekend lunches together. Sometimes I thought of my father and, with a wave of passionate loyalty, laid my slice of bread down.

"Eat it up," my mother said. "Think of those poor starving Belgian children."

The jelly was, all of it, superlative. My mother seemed not to have been able to make anything except well. But nowadays I can see how a glass of jelly is not quite the same thing as a charcoal drawing; for one thing, it is perishable.

I remember with pleasure the things my mother cooked, but I can also remember her doing it — how her face flushed to purple, how currants stained her hands, her hair fell in her eyes, and an expression of purpose tensed her face. If he caught her so, my father would be likely to say, "My dear, you are always the loveliest of your sex. But in that particular costume you look a little *less* lovely than I have ever seen you." The whole thing, all that cooking, caused him acute pain.

As I said, it was not just that he preferred her to look beautiful. It was also that her kitchen activities so often seemed to result in total exhaustion, when she lay supine on the bed, room darkened, a washcloth wrung out of cold water pressed to her brow. "I knew it would end in cry," my father would say grimly, as he visited the sickroom on his return at night from his studio.

Patrons of my mother's work would send presents to the exhausted artist: a bowl of delicate wine jelly, or lavender sachet to freshen the pillow. Mrs. Harcourt often sent her gleaming limousine to take my mother for a drive. *For she had been overdoing.* "Overdoing" was a word of fear, all through my youth. Attentions such as these made my father pull the corner of his mouth down, and I knew that he was thinking it unfair she should be considered domestically careworn, when he never wanted her to do all that cooking in the first place.

I knew he was thinking, Why must she insist on doing what the world does? The world had its ways, and my parents had theirs — a painters' life so precious, so joyful, that only a saying of Gainsborough's that my father loved adequately expresses it: "We are all going to Heaven, and Van Dyck is of the company." It seemed to my father that he and she had quite enough to do with the world as it was — attending to things that couldn't be got out of. Income tax forms, for one thing. What could be more tedious, less rewarding, and at the same time so alarming? My parents were convinced that the slightest slip in making out their forms would instantly result in severe and relentless punishment. Almost any March 14th — or more likely, March 13th — my father would come stamping into the house to snatch the long envelope he had come back for, thus missing his regular train, shouting, "Got to get this in the mail, or I shall go to state's prison."

Since practical matters were noxious, why can vegetables? The only thing my father ever wanted my mother to do was paint.

After he died, she began going through old trunks full of letters — of his and of his family's — up in the attic. She could even handle old letters with a style of her own. I can see her seated on a broken chair pulled up to the rim of a trunk, holding some letter before her eyes to read by the light from a dusty window, with that expression — grave, awed — she used when she read anything at all. Then she would tie the letters up into neat packets of equal size, using, to tie them, old material she had torn into narrow strips, to save string. I always can recognize any packet she tied by the tie — red-and-white gingham, or blue cotton, or green denim, or simply white sheeting; whatever she had on hand.

I used to protest, just as my father would have protested, that she was supposed to be an artist, and not a housewife.

"But who else will sort out all these wonderful letters from all those fascinating people?" she would cry. With the back of her hand she batted at the strand of wavy hair, silver white, that had fallen into her eyes. I could make no reply — I knew I would never do it.

Years later, when I formed my opinion about my mother's being by nature a practical rather than an artistic person, she had come to live near me in Virginia. "Ask some people to lunch," I would suggest. "Nobody makes a table look as pretty as you do. You could use your Dresden."

"I can't possibly invite anybody," my mother would very likely reply. "I've got Percy Hewer coming to pose every day at nine."

"Then ask them for dinner," I said.

"I shall be exhausted," she said firmly.

Nothing I ever said, it seemed to me then, made any difference to her. When she wanted to tie up old letters, she tied up old letters. When she didn't want people in, she didn't have them. "My mother is the most exasperating person in the world," I said once to an old lady who had known us both forever. "Stubborn as a mule."

"I know exactly what you mean," she said. "You can't do a thing with her but love her." I knew it was true, but I was not sure that I could.

When I used to go over to my mother's Virginia apartment, she never failed to greet me with open arms and cries of joy, as if she hadn't seen me for years. Then we would go and look at whatever drawing she'd been working on in the morning.

"Give me a crit," she would say.

I would summon the knowledge I imbibed as a child growing up in a family of painters and later in art school, and suggest where I thought an arm was out of drawing, where the foreshortening was off, or where a black accent was, I thought, needed.

"You're your papa's own child," she would say.

To talk to a parent, years after one has grown up, is as fascinating as being able to ask an author the questions his novel has stirred up.

"What was the matter with that maid we had, the one who kept calling 'Coo-coo . . . Coo-coo . . .' out of the window?" I might ask. Or, "What made Papa decide not to go and live in New York after all? He *said* life in New York was a lot easier for artists than in Boston." Or, "Why was William Rothenstein visiting us that time he scared me? Where did we know *him?*" Once, as we were drinking tea, I asked, "What made you do all that preserving and jelly-making, when I was a child? It used to upset Papa, you got so tired."

"I know, it was horrid of me," she said. "But you see it was the First World War."

"Papa thought you ought to stick to being an artist," I said.

"But President Wilson and Mr. Hoover said it was my duty!" she said, with wide, beautiful gray eyes. "They said I ought to save everything I could."

Instantly every reflex of my generation sprang up in me in battle array. "That's always been the trouble with you, doing what you ought to!" I exclaimed. "Why don't you ever do what you *want* to?"

My mother turned her forever-young regard — innocent of psychology, too noble for fashion — upon me. "But I want to do what I ought to do," she said.

TWO

The Loosening

Joyous Gard

WHEN I was clearing out the studio of the stone house by the sea that I inherited from my mother, the life once lived there seemed to get realer and realer until, when I would come in from a swim or a walk on the moors, on entering the studio I could smell distinctly not only the oil paint and turpentine from my mother's reign but, rising from layers of years upon years, the nitric acid used in solution to bite the etching plates of my old aunt, who had built the studio back in 1911.

Once or twice, to my astonishment, I burst into tears. What astonished me was not so much that I should be crying as what, I realized, I was crying about. It was not because my mother or Aunt Nelly was dead, or out of sadness for all those other artists, Aunt Nelly's friends, who also used the place long ago; but because, in the silence of the studio, I remembered what a wonderful time they had all had. Up to that moment it hadn't occurred to me that my aunt's old-maid existence could be considered as having a good time. Perhaps it was my fatigue, but all at once her life seemed as innocently paradisiacal as Dylan Thomas's Fern Hill — happy as the grass was green.

At the end of the nineteenth century, and especially in Boston, there were many what Henry James called Mighty Maidens, but those powerful figures had little to do with the kind of Boston spinster my Aunt Nelly was. She was neither an athlete, an organizer, a leader of society, nor rich. In fact I find it difficult to explain to anyone today how someone with as little as she, could ever have built and had the possessions to fill that big studio.

She was born in 1855, well within a hundred years of the founding of the Republic. The running of the government, politics, appeared to her in the light of intimate, everyday, almost family concerns. While keeping house for her father when he was Chaplain of the Senate, she became friends with Mrs. Theodore Roosevelt and Mrs. Gifford Pinchot, and made a drawing of the President in his office that radiates Teddy's famous gusto. Some painters might have parlayed those years into a position of power, or at least of privilege; but not my Aunt Nelly.

She was blithe as a bird, but the bird was Job's turkey. Her income was literally derived from funds presented to her mother by her father's grateful congregation at the time of his death. She had, in addition, a set of highly unworldly principles to support her. Insofar as she possessed any rigidity at all — she was about as rigid as a withered clove pink — it was toward the idea of personal power as a positive value. One of the few times I ever saw her angry was when I was a young girl visiting her by the sea and a Harvard cousin told us about one of his golden friends who'd been arrested for a whole complex of driving offenses. He told us of all he and his classmates were doing to get the youth off. It seemed the arresting officer had made some technical slip, which might serve . . .

"You mean your friend was not guilty of the charges?" Aunt Nelly said. Her old and slightly simian face looked puzzled.

"Oh, sure," my cousin said. "But he's such a wonderful guy! So gifted. Such an unusual guy, just full of love. . . ."

"If he were really a fine young man, he would *long* to uphold the law," Aunt Nelly said.

Likewise, the only time I ever saw her violent, was standing watching a parade in Washington. A man in front of us didn't take his hat off when the flag went by along Pennsylvania Avenue. Aunt Nelly raised her black cotton umbrella and knocked it off. I remember how, at the age of seventeen, it embarrassed me.

The annual celebration of Fourth of July at Aunt Nelly's on Cape Ann was one of the few attractions ever to draw my father away, if only for the weekend, from his Boston studio. His two remaining brothers used to come, too, the professor and the railroad man — the latter the only member of the family with social aspirations, which were no more referred to by the rest of the family than if they had been his

Mongolian idiot child. My father did remark to me once, "Your Uncle Arthur is *proud* of being able to put up at his own club in almost every city in the country," but he said it in tones of wonder.

The house, gray and shingled, where we stayed in those days was named The Thickets after the wild plums in front. It had once been a fisherman's cottage. When my aunt and Miss Clements, the artist with whom she lived, bought it to summer in with their old mothers, they moved it up from the road, turned it around, and added a studio. The front piazza faced the sea. After breakfast on the Fourth, everyone went out there in the salt-smelling sunshine. The big flag was flying from the piazza roof.

The custom, based on memories of my Grandfather Hale, was for Uncle Arthur to read the Declaration slowly, giving plenty of time for the others to punctuate it by smashing torpedoes on the piazza floor. It made a satisfying ritual. My mother stood to one side like some great white flower, petals melting in the sun, looking uncomprehending. Her own tradition was quite different, almost Tory; rooted in family memories of England. Instead of that enormous figure Van Wyck Brooks has described as resembling an untidy Pilgrim Father, the father *she* had to remember was shattered in health, tortured with worry concerned with the sale of gunsights to foreign governments, exhausted, dying.

One Fourth of July Aunt Nelly, at all times given to a nervous habit of rubbing her fingers together as though working a piece of artist's kneaded rubber, kept rubbing two torpedoes together and, naturally, got burned. It was just like her. My father claimed he once asked her what she would do if there was a fire and she was trapped in an upstairs bedroom.

"I'd make a rope out of the bedsheets," she replied sensibly.

"And then what?"

"Why, I'd tie one end to the bedpost, go to the window with the other end in my hand, and jump."

Stoop-shouldered, skinny as a shadow, wearing high black laced boots, she used to dash about The Thickets at such a rate that Lizzie Doonan, the Irish maid my grandmother got off the boat as a girl in the eighties, would cry, "Ah, Miss Nally, she's runnin' like the wild deer!"

Aunt Nelly studied painting under Carolus Duran in the Paris of the seventies. By the time I knew her, any money she made from her work came from etchings, and from commissions for enormous church decorations. She had to climb up a stepladder to work on the upper reaches of them. It was a miracle that she never fell off, but she did thump down on her knees so often, working on the lower parts, that she acquired chronic housemaid's knee. Winding the bandages around her legs in the mornings took forever, and by the time I came into the picture she had consented, much against her disposition, to let Lizzie bring her breakfast in bed.

The rest of us used to breakfast in the sunny white dining room from which you could see the ocean waiting, through one open door, and the garden with its red and white roses climbing up locust posts, through the other. Miss Clements and whatever old-maid painter friends might be visiting were always filled with energy in the morning, but my mother drooped like a white rose over her cup of tea and the muffin she crumbled and did not eat.

She was always exhausted when we first arrived at The Thickets, with that mysterious exhaustion — that disease of fatigue — thwarting her every active impulse at home and haunting my childhood. On winter afternoons, when I got home from school, she was often lying down, face flushed, a cold compress on her forehead. Her large gray eyes met mine piteously as I entered the darkened bedroom.

"I'm all tuckered out," she would say, trying to joke. "I've had to cave in."

It was as if some fearful presence hovered around her, menacing, evil, waiting to pounce the minute she left the magic circle of her morning's work. To me, as a child, that presence seemed almost real: harsh, male, cruelly demanding. But my mother and I lived alone in our house at the edge of the woods with my father — tired, gentle, and romantic. There was nobody else.

At The Thickets she began to perk up. Something about the life there braced her like a tart New England tonic. Even after hours of painting, she still had the energy to take a walk with me up past the fishhouses, or to sit on the beach playing with pebbles while I swam in the icy waves. She herself never went into the water. By the middle of our visit, she was taking helpings of creamed codfish and hominy for breakfast, and when we got home again, our visit beside the sea sustained her for weeks before the dreadful shadow again descended.

I used to notice how, at The Thickets, not only my father but all the old maids watched my mother at breakfast, fascinated, as though she were some rare and precious flower, different from them. Perhaps it was because she was much the most talented among them; also, my mother was a different — a solitary — kind of painter. Close to her, I had experienced art as a lonely, mystical pursuit; here at Aunt Nelly's for the first time I saw art lived corporately — a shared vocation to be embarked on daily with cries of joy.

When I finished eating breakfast I used to go up and sit on the edge of Aunt Nelly's bed. If she wasn't lying back reading the New Testament, she would be sitting up winding Ace bandages round and round her thin shanks. A self-portrait painted when she was thirty-five, wearing a bonnet, against a bluish background that, with its fishlike streaks of green, resembled the bottom of the sea, shows her face was not unlovely. She must have had offers. But her middle years were given up to looking after a semi-invalid mother and a famous, sought-after, impractical, extrovert father. By him, and by her mother — who was not, like my mother's mother, so much horrified and outraged by what she found in marriage as simply, after nine children, worn out by it — Aunt Nelly was sorely needed to keep house, be hostess, and fend the circling harpies off him and the well-intentioned parishioners off her.

I used to fly into a rage when my mother sometimes suggested that it must have been wonderful to have such a devoted daughter. Was not Aunt Nelly the epitome of that worst of all fates, sex starvation? A human sacrifice upon the altar of filial duty?

"I don't see why everybody feels they have to get married and have children, just like *sheep*," my mother said. "I think Aunt Nelly's life has been beautiful. So innocent and unconscious of self."

To my mother, innocent and unconscious were words of high praise, but with my generation they were unfashionable, to put it mildly. Nobody really *was* innocent, for one thing.

Once my grandparents were dead Aunt Nelly's life, what was left of it, became her own. The first thing she did was to build, with borrowed money, the stone studio — a short walk up from The Thickets; it was to remain heavily mortgaged for the rest of her life. Besides a working place of her own, it provided room for the accumulation she'd inherited: in addition to an alcove for the etching press and space for her enormous easels, the classical library of a great-uncle, Edward Everett the orator; stacks of engravings brought back by every member of the family who went abroad, much as today people bring back slides; cupboards for the family toys — besides the doll's four-poster, the doll's crinoline and wired calash, there were Lotto, blocks, old books for children; and hundreds and hundreds of family letters running back into the eighteenth century.

Once Aunt Nelly's bandages were securely wound, her thin gray hair looped up and confined by a black velvet "headache band," and she was dressed in long black cloth skirt and black shirtwaist, with a number of silver chains around her neck from which hung seals, keys, and the watch she tucked into her waistband, she was ready to set off, uttering cries, for the new studio. Everything Aunt Nelly did was accompanied by cries — of departure, of arrival, of welcome. Her work required a great many models, whom she found among the neighborhood, and I think of her studio as always filled with people. My friends up there today include persons I first encountered dressed as Mary or Joseph, as an angel or a shepherd. I pay taxes on a quarry I own jointly with the erstwhile Baby Jesus.

In the afternoons she would garden, so passionately that occasionally she broke something — a wrist, a collarbone. There was much gardening to do. The lawns had borders of delphinium and lupine, sweet William and bleeding heart; rock gardens lined the two paths leading from the lower house to the upper. Aunt Nelly called the lower path — the one everybody used — the *escalier de service;* it was one of her tiny jokes. She had made a water garden out of the hole that the stone for the studio came out of. Mallows and water lilies abounded in it, and the cardinal flowers that my professor uncle brought back to plant in it, from his walks over the moors. Large goldfish swam lazily round its pool of water. As I wandered with my mother down the rough stone steps, a bullfrog leapt off the lily pad where he had been sunning, plop.

We ate supper by the light, unnecessary till dessert, of candles with blue-and-white shades. Their flames trembled in a salt breeze from the door on the sea. If flies came in, the custom was to make an organized assault on them. Everyone rose and, waving big dinner napkins, drove them out of the garden door and shut it after them. Against the wall a low dresser held blue-and-white china: onion pattern, willow, and Canton. Aunt Nelly, Miss Clements, and their painter friends were like Whistler deeply influenced by the Japanese and by blue-and-white.

Aunt Nelly's brothers felt considerable resistance to Miss Clements. My father told me that when his sister announced their plan to share a house, years before, he warned her, "Don't do it. She's a juggernaut. She'll flatten you out." He was not given to expressing antipathies any more overtly than that. He had his own complicated system for registering disapproval, which only the initiated — my mother and I — recognized. He himself, for instance, felt an epoch-making moment in his relation with Miss Clements had been reached one Fourth of July when, at supper — she having asserted some opinion in her loud, confident voice — he said, "There, Gabrielle, we differ." I feel sure Miss Clements didn't even realize an epoch had been made.

Aunt Nelly sat, silent, at the foot of the table opposite Miss Clements; visitors to the sides. She would help herself to steamed clams on a Friday evening, to baked beans and brown bread on a Saturday, but what she did was to stir them round and round with her fork. She would lift a forkful and hold it in midair while she listened to one of Miss Clements' long and lively stories. (One reason that lady jarred so on my father was that he, too, was a great story-teller, and her stories competed with his.) After a while, Aunt Nelly's fork would go, not up to her lips, but back to her plate. I used to watch, fascinated, to see if I could catch her eating anything. In principle she was fond of cod — less, I suspect, as food than out of sentiment for the position in Massachusetts' economy over the centuries that had rendered it sacred. She had quite a personal feeling for cod. Once, in the low, quiet voice she used for saying anything funny, she remarked that a cod, new caught, mouth gaping, looks as if it were saying, "And has it come to this!"

After dinner we read aloud or to ourselves in the white-walled parlor. Until only a short time before my aunt died she could not afford to put electricity in either of the houses. In the granite house, which she gave my mother after my father died, we didn't have any till around 1940. We read by the steady light of kerosene lamps — big standing lamps, or squat ones set on a table, with rounded green glass shades. Sometimes the lamps smoked — a thin black streak ascending — and had to be turned down until the flame spread evenly across the wick. Smoking blackened the chimneys, which had in any case to be cleaned daily by Lizzie Doonan.

When we went to bed we each took a candle from the table at the foot of the white-painted square staircase. The brass candlesticks, with their wide saucers, had a snuffer attached to one side, and a loop for the thumb on the other. We trailed slowly up the stairs while Aunt Nelly dashed about downstairs closing doors and emitting cries of good night. Our shadows leaped ahead of us. When my mother and I were inside the white bedroom we shared, with only the sound that the sea made slapping against the rocks, the shadows would mount the walls mysteriously as we undressed.

Sometimes neighbors came in for the evening. The occasions were various clubs my aunt and her friends formed — a knitting club during the First World War, a French club. Old sisters and wives of Yankee fishermen, sturdy Finnish women whose fathers migrated in the last century to work the quarries, sat knitting and listening to one of their number read aloud. I'm sure it was Aunt Nelly's idea, wanting Finns to read French. Her blue-stockinghood was fortified by a flair for languages. Besides Latin and some Greek, she knew Italian, a little Spanish from Santa Barbara winters, and spoke French fluently with a Boston accent. At the age of seventy-odd she learned enough Finnish to pay her friends the compliment of reading the Kalevala.

At nine o'clock Lizzie came in with lemonade and thin ginger cookies.

"A real tasty cookie, Miss Hale," old Miss Hattie Bates, whose brother showed me my first whale through his spyglass, would remark.

But before Aunt Nelly could say a word Miss Clements would, as usual, reply. "Yes, they *are* delicious, aren't they? *We* think so." It was not at all what Aunt Nelly would have said.

Whether from innate gentleness, good manners, or lack of energy, she, unlike my father, never even differed with Miss Clements. Years after her death, when I was sightseeing in Charleston, I met an elderly gentleman etcher who had known her there, and who said, "Your aunt had one of the most delightful and diverting minds I ever encountered. But such a time I had getting to talk to her! That woman was always interrupting."

When I burst into tears that summer it came to me, however, that even my father could accept Miss Clements in the light of what a good time they all had painting. On his Fourth of July weekends he made one of the procession that set out, workward, after breakfast, accompanied by Aunt

Nelly's cries of joy — he to paint pochade seascapes of wild roses against pink granite, viridian water with a white triangle of sail, gray slash of gull against cobalt sky. He could be seen all morning over on the Point, in his white shirt and stiff collar, behind a borrowed sketching easel, as he set pointillist dots of pure color on his tiny board — faithful, persistent, resigned to disappointment. When he came home for lunch he would look around at the faces at the table, all of them filled with the same inner satisfaction at the morning spent. "We'd ought to call this place Joyous Gard," he said once. "Out of Malory."

The others would have trooped up to what continued to be called the new studio. If a church decoration was under way, Miss Clements and the other old maids might all work on it — painting great oranges, like burning orbs, high on the Tree of Life, or many-colored flowers in the Palestinian grass — while Aunt Nelly worked on the circle of radiance around the Child. Another year it might be etchings they worked on. Their plates had generally been drawn upon earlier, in Charleston, Baltimore, Girgenti, the Holy Land, wherever they'd wintered; if drypoints, with a ruby or diamond on bare copper that didn't need etching; if a true etching, on applied soft or hard grounds. My mother never made etchings anywhere but here; she would be sitting to one side, her Italianate profile bent gravely over the covered soft-ground she drew on with a special needle.

I sat with a book in my lap and watched. The old ladies gave themselves to "process" — the preparing and printing of plates — with a peculiar, gay intensity. In their eccentric garb they hurried about the huge studio, lowering a plate into the nitric acid bath by means of a cradle made of string; applying black ink to an etched plate with a rag-covered roller, or colored inks to an aquatint — printed similarly except that spaces instead of lines were etched, to give an effect like watercolor. All together — my mother, too — they might print a take, one of them with infinite care setting a plate face down upon wet paper on a padded bed, another slowly, slowly turning the spokes of the great wheel as it moved the platen over the bed; another taking notes throughout to record each step of the process, so a final edition could be printed uniformly. Afterward they all clustered around to examine critically the result achieved. The atmosphere — brisk, fresh, precise — was permeated by the smell of the nitric acid bath.

One day at lunch a tiny, desiccated Miss Leslie Jackson told us that when she had proposed painting some sunset or other her teacher, the then-famous Frank Benson, said not to — that sunsets were impossible as a subject. At supper Aunt Nelly produced the following lines, spoken in her quietest voice:

> Said Leslie Jackson to Mr. Benson,
> "Yon sunset merits your attention."
> "That's the kind we turn our backs on!"
> Said Mr. Benson to Leslie Jackson.

After years of minor accidents, the magic protecting madmen, children, and Aunt Nelly seemed to run out. When she was nearing eighty she fell, while running in the studio like the wild deer, and broke her hip. In those days a broken hip meant, for most elderly people, prompt death from pneumonia, but my frail old aunt somehow managed to continue painting from a wheelchair, giving little cries of painter's satisfaction, and to keep up through the newspapers and her correspondence with politics and the government.

Prohibition was still in force. In winter, after the old ladies had gone away, the stone studio, The Thickets, and the other shingled houses, weathered to matchbox dryness, that friends over the years had bought or rented, were boarded up. The cove the houses overlooked became a favorite landing for boats running liquor down from Canada. In June, houseowners often found their rooms littered with the straw bottles had been packed in. I was in my twenties, and I well remember the respectfully wide berth everyone gave bootleggers, rumrunners, and the proprietors of speakeasies. Bootlegging was a fact of life no one argued with.

One winter Aunt Nelly got word, I think from the Finnish pastor, that rumrunners were using the shed behind the stone studio for signaling to incoming boats. She didn't hesitate an instant. She wrote off, giving instructions for the shed to be burned down at once. Her luck must have returned, for neither her house nor any of the others was burned in retaliation.

Aunt Nelly died in a nursing home in the eighty-sixth year of her age and the one hundred and sixty-fourth of the republic. My father was long dead by then, but my mother looked after her with the devotion she showed for all my father's family, going to see her — a distance of ten miles — every day. The nurses in the home adored Aunt Nelly, for even when she was wandering in her mind she never failed in her exquisite politeness and consideration, the sweetness of her temper, her happiness that was like the happiness in Paradise before the paternal ordinance was breached and Satan's shadow loomed.

With all her jauntings about the world, Aunt Nelly's essence — her original, young girl's ardor — remained intact. It was as if the patriarchal figure of her father had sufficed her, and she never needed to break the law. Instead of rebelling, she dashed to meet an old maid's fate with cries of consent. I see how I could, when exhausted, weep for the cool white cloisters Aunt Nelly built out of her inheritance; they seemed like a jail to me when I was young, but what my memory has retained is their freshness, their peace, their self-sufficiency.

My mother used to drive me over to the nursing home when I would come up from New York to spend the weekend with her. I had never seen anyone dying before, and I was struck by the signs of Aunt Nelly's physical dissolution. As she lay on her side in bed, increasingly her emaciated, battered old knees were being drawn toward her bony chest until, the last time I saw her, she was totally and irrevocably curled up, as though grotesquely illustrating, in that antique frame, the child born of a virgin she had painted on canvas so often. It was hardly an apotheosis of her life, much less a promise of richer life to come, but a sort of literal exposition of life's core.

Inheriting a Garden

AMONG self-portraits of my mother that I fell heir to is a charcoal study for the painting required by the National Academy of Design as an initiation, on the occasion of her election to membership. The drawing reveals how my mother felt it necessary to pose herself — looking over her shoulder at a foreshortened angle to minimize what she thought of as her awful, jutting chin, her hook-y nose. She holds the stick of charcoal up and gazes with an artist's calculating stare at her reflection in a pier glass that is outside the picture.

In the end her self-deprecation has turned into a sort of surprise present, one of the many I keep turning up as if they were real packages she had left tucked away in corners of real drawers. For, when I am appalled by what has befallen the face I see in the mirror, as she must sometimes have been, I realize that things are not necessarily as bad as they seem. When I was a young girl and beaux came to call, they used to take one look at my mother and settle down to serious courting, assured of the future of my appearance. Now those despairs of my mother's give me confidence that my own looks, though lesser, may last out.

She wasn't a cosseter of her beauty. Although she was capable of taking an hour and half to dress for a party and emerge from her room looking like a duchess, very often when she had finished her morning's painting she used to spend the rest of the Cape Ann summer day gardening in an old striped seersucker dress, her feet in torn, discarded espadrilles of mine, a bandanna faded pale red tying her hair down, with her deplorable jaw set, as she dug out dandelions and sorrel. Her gardening was unsparing. During droughts, she carried water in a pail, since the town forbade sprinkling or even, in extremities, any use of the hose at all; she sawed off dead limbs, forked over the compost heap, nailed up high gray driftwood supports for the Paul's Scarlet roses to clamber over.

"Come and help me!" she used to cry; though not so often after years of my making it plain I did not want to.

I had in mind more sybaritic summers, like the pictures in *Vogue*. "Why don't we let it all run to lovely field grass?" I said.

A look of passionate distress twisted her features — stained with sweat, streaked with dirt where she'd slapped a mosquito, but still, like an old statue's, beautiful.

"It wouldn't be the way you imagine," she said. "Nature can't just be left like that."

The standard for her gardening afternoons was the same as for her painting mornings — quite simply, perfection. And in the early mornings when the cove lay green and glassy-still at the bottom of the hill, and the dew left pocket handkerchiefs spread on the garden grass to dry, and gulls flew, hoarsely crying, to the sea, the garden seemed one of those places where a secret of nature has been trapped, like the river garden within the portaled wall of a willow plate, and that must always be returned to if the secret is to be re-experienced.

After my mother's death it seemed imperative that her garden should not be allowed to disintegrate. It appeared too well established, too structurally conformed to the land's contour to need more than custodial care. She had used the outcroppings of native granite as part of her design. The stone walls that the terrace was bordered with were put in years ago by a Finn who took his work as hard as she took hers; he told her he couldn't sleep for worry about getting the curve of the wall right. Also part of her design were the tall bare locusts, like bleached bones, an occasional glacial boulder, and the indigenous bushes — beach plum, sassafras, and sweet fern. The summer after my mother died, I weeded my way through my grief, pulling out sorrel blindly with my fingers instead of digging it out, propelled by the compulsion to preserve instead of to abandon her creation.

In close relationships, it takes discernment to distinguish which qualities belong to whom, and I never before quite took it in — that all the gardening in our lives had been done entirely by my mother. To watch people gardening, to listen to them talk, even though endlessly, about gardening, to help weed, is not to garden. My ignorance turned out to be, in fact, almost total.

I stood by the back door with the longest clippers in my hands, trying to reach the grapevine that floated out in long streamers above the windows. She was right — you could not leave nature alone a single season. Thick stems of ivy had worked themselves into the cracks of the door and window frames, and ivy pushed between the granite steps, separating them.

The supports for the roses had had to be taken down when the kitchen wing was reroofed, and how was I ever to get them up again? Nobody thought, while they were being removed, to see how they had been attached. The carpenter said they couldn't be nailed to the gutters without causing leaks. Somehow they must be firmly fixed or the winter gales would bring them and the roses down.

The dandelions on the lawn were coming up thicker than ever, and it was too much to keep the wide beds of Rosa Mundae roses weeded, on top of everything else, though their pink-and-white stripes were among the sights I loved best. The magic was leaking out of the garden. When I looked at the terrace I thought of the sorrel between the stones. The winding stone steps meant grass cuttings in crevices; the yellow Scotch roses meant weeds in where the thorns scratched my wrists; the crab apple trees meant dead limbs to prune. The remains of the delphinium and the irises in the border meant further weeding. And the climbing yellow rose beside the front steps had died.

I sat on the stone wall, at the hour when the light on the rocks around the cove turns violet and the gulls fly out to sea to follow fishing boats home, cornered by the pass to which my own insistence on staying ignorant had brought me.

Now I could see how much my mother knew that I didn't know and never would know — there wasn't time any more to learn it as she had learned it — and I asked myself whether there was any point in trying to preserve the garden. Why not let the whole thing run to field grass, after all? I tried to remember whether gardening had ever meant anything to me, or whether it had all of it belonged to her. But my mind, instead, went back to winter, in the old house in Dedham where I grew up.

It was like dreaming to remember how hard the winters were to get through. The living room and the dining room needed their fireplaces going to make them livable. On the north side of the house, my father's study and my mother's studio stayed cold. The Franklin stove did get lighted in the study after dinner, when my father went there to draw for the rest of the evening, but the studio never warmed up.

Sometimes the pipes froze, and we had no water except what we could carry in buckets from a neighbor's and store in the bathtub and the oval copper canning boiler.

The maid was responsible for feeding the kitchen stove, banking it at night, and opening the drafts to bring it to life in the morning. Our ancient, peculiar hired man — who, when he chopped wood, could be heard muttering, "If the logs had heads, I'd chop 'em off" — kept the wood baskets by the fireplaces filled with logs. My mother never came in from outdoors without an armful of fagots for kindling. But my father was responsible for the furnace, which he hated. Early in the morning before he left for his studio, he shook it down and stoked it. As soon as he got home at

night it had to be attended to. And in the evenings, when I
had gone to bed and was nearly asleep, I would hear him
clumping slowly down the cellar stairs and, a minute later,
the scrape of the coal shovel. Sometimes he struck his head
against the low-running pipes. "God damn it to hell!" he
would exclaim. I could hear him all the way up two flights of
stairs. It shocked my mother to death, but she hadn't the heart
to scold him. I lay still in bed, stricken with his despair.

He used to cheer himself up by the use of a number of slogans he repeated to me as we plowed through a mile of
road together after breakfast, on blizzardy mornings, he to
the station, I to school.

"Get the men forward anyhow," was one of my extremely
unmilitary father's slogans. "Be the day short or be it long,
At length it cometh to evensong," was another. Dressed in
shabby overcoat, galoshes, and the bowler hat he wore because, he said, he wanted to look not like an artist but a stock-
broker, he stumped grimly through the falling snow, one
corner of his mouth jerked down under his walrus mustache.
In closest communion with his thoughts as we plowed along
past the buried fences, I suffered with him.

I remember one particular dun-colored, snowy morning
when the winter was at its bitterest. We were passing the
Shrivers' high stone wall, and he had just finished telling
me, "Don't you care about those nasty little girls at school;
when you grow up everything will get better. You'll see." I
looked at the stone wall with snow clinging in its myriad
crevices, and tried to imagine what it would be like to
grow up and not get called names like Walking Diction-
ary, or not to care if I was called them. It was then that
my father said, his voice changing as he changed the

subject, "What do you think. *The first seed catalogue came!*"

I felt a great flood of relief. All manner of thing was going to be all right, after all; not only for me but for him. We continued walking to the village in the snow, my hand in his.

In late January and early February, seed catalogues would pour thick and fast through the letter slot under one of the narrow windows that flanked the front door. Breck's, Farquhar's, Burpee's, Ferry's — I have forgotten the names of all the nurseries, but not the change that their catalogues meant. My parents now spent their evenings poring over them. My mother was selecting annuals for the border, sedums for the rock garden, replacements for climbing roses in the lower garden that had died, grass seed for bare spots in the lawn. My father was what he called "looking out" vegetables. When Daylight Saving Time began, in the First World War, it might have been solely to give my father pleasure. His commitment to painting kept him at his studio till time to catch the train home for dinner, but now he could look forward in good conscience to long summer evenings tending his green flesh melons and his asparagus bed, his corn hills and his strawberries.

As for me, I sat up as long as I was allowed, joyfully hunting up the radishes in all the catalogues — scarlet globe radishes, white icicles. Radishes were my specialty, because they came up faster than anything else. Other vegetables required patience, of which I had none. When I stuck radish seeds in the ground, before I knew it up would pop a row of little, round, twin leaves.

More than choosing seeds my headiest pleasure, those snowbound evenings, was in looking at the pictures — seed-

catalogue art, showing the grass-green pods opened to reveal perfect peas like green teeth; the fat tomatoes of bright
scarlet, purple pansies big as a plate, exactly perfect roses in
pink, yellow, or crimson, spires of mammoth snapdragon,
ears of Golden Bantam corn bursting from green husks, Ken-
tucky Wonder beans, royal purple beets, great headed-up
cabbages, delirious strawberries of crimson buttoned down
with yellow seeds. Like no other pictures they could awak-
en hopes of a better and infinitely desirable world.

In no time, snowdrops were hanging pearl-drop heads
under the living-room windows. Mr. Davey, the greenhouse
man, who was an elderly Scot, was engaged ahead of time
to plow the lower garden. Now all was promise, and as I
walked home from school one day I would see our town's
other old Scotsman marching along the country road all
alone, playing the bagpipes as he always did as soon as
spring was in the air. There he comes, up past Lowder
Brook, dressed in kilt, socks, and sporran, lifting his knees
high in military advance and intent upon the production of
his loud and lonely lament.

Empty places — a vacuum where something once has been
— draw the eye and obsess the imagination. That afternoon,
sitting on the stone wall, I kept staring at the bare spot next
to the granite front steps where my mother's rose had died.
Its great blossoms used to drop like yellow velvet on the
stone. Now nothing grew between the steps and the angle
of the living-room alcove except a few Black-eyed Susans.
It occurred to me I would like to plant a red rose there.

I wouldn't have known there could follow, out of me,
such an outcry. How my mother would have *hated* the ob-

viousness of red rose against gray stone! Her taste was better than mine any day: she saw things with an outward eye, where I could only imagine. Not only was it safer to follow her lead in taste, and buy another Mrs. Arthur Curtis James, but, if I wanted to preserve my mother's garden, that was how to preserve it.

I went to find some old seed catalogues I had stuck in a big pile under the model stand in the studio when they came, not knowing what else to do with them. The pages devoted to roses looked just the way they had years ago. I needed a yellow climber for that granite wall, but the one called Crimson Glory was what I had to have. In the picture it had shadows of purplish black, and its petals rolled back upon themselves at the edges — a perfect rose, deep heart and mystic shape. It had to be a red rose against gray stone, I couldn't help it, that was what I wanted. Old, wild, forgotten hopes woke in my mind, as of a paragon blooming, an apotheosis of roses — although in fact I didn't even know how to plant it. I would have to look it up in the dog-eared garden book my mother left behind in her wicker gardening basket, along with scratcher, secateur, and trowels. I would have to get some bone meal to put in the hole.

I would probably plant it wrong, too. It would very likely die. But my mother's yellow rose died too, and what she would have hated most of all would be to have her garden stop growing.

These summer mornings when I get up and go into the stone kitchen, I make myself a cup of coffee and carry it into the garden, where the birds are flying in low sweeps. From the garden chair I can see the cove below — green, still, and glassy. The tips of the irises I transplanted last year make a spiky fringe against the water; I found they throve on being banged around. Weeds still flourish between the stones of the terrace, and just to look at them is to remember my mother crouched on her little round gardening stool, the pale-red kerchief binding her head, tirelessly digging them out.

But I am too lazy to do that, and, contrary to all my fears, the sedums and the moss seem year by year to be overcoming the sorrel. The Crimson Glory I planted is thriving—and so are the Paul's Scarlet roses, red against gray stone, that were of course part of my mother's planting all along. But there is no doubt this garden is not as good a garden as it was *sub regno* my mother.

The garden casts a hush in early morning, as if some old forgotten secret were being silently exposed once more. Terminus—the weather-pocked Greek statue a great-uncle brought back from Alexandria—sits as ever among irises and columbine, staring blindly out to sea. The white maple a neighbor predicted would die has doubled its size in three years, and waves large, silver-green leaves in the little breeze. Instinct says, Do nothing; stay perfectly still; barely breathe.

But there is danger everywhere. At any moment, something can filter through the green wall of leaves, or the blue wall towards the sea—aphis, green worms that drop by a thread, earwigs, a driving rain to penetrate the windowsills, the ivy under the threshold. At every portal, fortify with shears and secateur, with spray gun and worn-out Turkish towels, to hedge around—*set free?*—what's trapped within this place.

The World, the Flesh,
and the Devil

SHORTLY before my mother died, a friend came up to me on the street and said she had been horrified by something my mother told her. (My friend is a lapsed Catholic and very shockable in reverse.) What my mother had said was that she found the developments of the space age profoundly distressing since they demonstrated to her incontrovertibly that heaven was not out there, hence my father could not be in it, hence she would not meet him there as she had always hoped to do.

One reason this confession shocked my friend may have been that my mother always looked so urbane and sophisticated that people couldn't grasp her special brand of innocence. She looked like a great lady who has been everywhere and done everything and whom nothing can shock. Actually she was often shocked. She canceled her subscription to *Life* on account of what she considered its salacious photographs. When I was young, one of my many attempts at reforming her used to consist of telling her about any friends of mine who strayed from the paths of virtue. I hoped by this means to accustom her to the modern world.

But she would only flush. "How disgusting!" she exclaimed.

Much later it dawned on me that she never turned against anybody whose behavior had thus offended her, however. At the time this only seemed to me an evidence of inconsistency.

"If you thought Daphne was so awful going off to Barbados, what are you being so nice to her for?" I might cross-question her after a party.

"But I'm fond of Daphne," she said, puzzled.

For the most part, she would not recognize the possibility of error in those whom she admired. Men who were gentle and feminine, for instance, she considered merely sensitive — the way a man ought to be. If, in my passion for her enlightenment, I suggested anything other, she would repulse the suggestion.

"I don't believe it," she would say. "There couldn't be anything so disgusting."

Above all, she held my father and my father's family perfect. I always knew she loved and revered them, but I didn't really take in the extent of what she felt until near the end of her life.

"It must have been awfully hard on Papa, being his father's son," I happened to say.

"Yes, having a famous father *is* hard on the children," she said.

"But I mean Grandpa was so dominating. It seems to me he wanted to be Jehovah and have everybody else do what he wanted. Look how exhausted Grandmamma was."

My mother cried out. When she cried out, you could see how heroines in novels of the last century had been intended to look. Her lovely face flushed, her eyes looked stricken, and her hands flew up like birds from whatever they were doing. "You never knew your grandfather or you couldn't say anything so dreadfully untrue!"

"He must have had *some* faults," I insisted. "Everybody has faults."

"Your grandfather didn't," she said positively. "Or your grandmother. Neither did your Aunt Nelly. The Hales didn't have any faults."

In actual cases of lesser, peccant humanity, my mother was gentle and forgiving. The first person ever deputed to take me walking, for instance, was — not a nurse, of course, in our impoverished artist's family, but a ravishing, subtly beautiful girl, during rest periods in posing for my mother. This was Carrie, a Boston artists' model. Her beauty was recherché; coppery, clinging hair, naughty eyes, bee-stung lip, tiptilted nose. My recollection of her is of a wild and lively spirit walking beside me up Sandy Valley Road in Dedham, who called the stones in the road dragon's teeth, and led me into a deep-green flower-starred clearing in the woods and named it the secret garden.

Carrie's presence in the house where I grew up was the last holdover from my parents' life in their Boston studio, before their decision to bring up their child — me — in the country. My childhood was enlivened by renditions of the music-hall songs, and the Yiddish or Irish jokes, that she used to sing and tell them while posing in the old days. My father used to say that if someone took her to an opera or a musical comedy, she would come to the studio next day and sing the whole score. He said she might have sung professionally, only she could never afford the training.

When my mother moved her studio to the country, such was their old attachment that for several years Carrie used to come all the way out from town to pose for her. It meant half an hour's train trip, and a mile walk from the station. Then, when I was about six, she disappeared from our lives. I was told she got fat. Even to a child it seemed incredible — that wildwood creature! Years later when I was grown up, I learned why she got fat and of the ensuing responsibilities which stopped her posing.

My mother told me about it in a tentative, deprecatory way. "Poor Carrie," she said. "She couldn't withstand that dreadful man." Carrie's fate seemed to cause no conflict in my mother's mind, however, with the principle she held that it was disgusting to think there was ever anything questionable about artists' models. Models were wonderful, she said; high-spirited girls with the gumption to make their own living.

And I remember her showing me, with a serious, exalted expression, a reproduction of Ingres's "La Source," and impressing upon me that the nude is something beautiful, pure, and essential to art. It was evident from the way she spoke that other people thought otherwise. Other people meant laymen. In the world I grew up in, laymen represented the devil. There was the world — wide, ravishing, and infinitely paintable; there were the artists, who painted the world in all its beauty and no more saw evil in it than a child would; and then there were laymen. The sniggering, the smutty jokes, the innuendos about artists' models and the nude all came from laymen. Laymen as a class not only didn't know anything about art but didn't want to — they scorned art.

Since art was highest on the scale of all existing values, the idea that anybody could look down on it, however mistakenly, made another convolution in the complicated balancing act that, as the child of artists, I had to perform.

As I walked along beside my father on the way to school, he used to tell me stories of his Paris days. Once my father made the decision to go to Paris, he was left, by his father, to his own devices. He supported himself there almost wholly by copying Old Masters; it brought a certain income from tourists who wanted to take a picture home from Europe without paying very much for it. He stayed a long time in Paris. A photograph of him at that time shows him lounging sidewise in a chair; his head is thrown back dashingly, but his eyes are anxious. He must have felt he *had* to be a success, after staking his judgment against the Jovian one. When he came back to America, about 1895, a show of his paintings at Durand-Ruel's caused a sensation with their pure Impressionism. He never followed up his New York success, however. He went back to Boston.

I loved his evocations of a life, carefree in its poverty-strickenness, among the camaraderie of the ateliers, the cafés, the hole-in-the-wall lodgings of the Left Bank. My father lived with two friends, in the rue des Saints-Pères, in a garret reached by a ladder nailed against the wall, up which he professed to have been able to climb carrying a lighted lamp and a pitcher of water. *"Philippe!"* one of his friends would roar. *"Voulez-vous apporter moi l'eau chaud ou voulez-vous nong?"* Since my father was in Paris during the eighties and nineties, those stories of his were much like the life in *Trilby* and *La Bohème*. When I got older and read the du Maurier book and heard the opera, it was with an almost personal nostalgia. *"O soave fanciulla"* brought back a life of youth and courage, at one remove from my own, it is true, but such a slight remove as to be the merest tissue: the distinction between my father and myself.

I knew, although I was a child, or perhaps because I was a child, that there was something naughty about that life that was delightful too. My father often told me stories that needed some explanation. Sometimes it was only the French that needed explaining, as in a song that he said was a favorite with the students:

> *La peinture à l'huile*
> *C'est bien difficile,*
> *Mais c'est bien plus beau*
> *Que la peinture à l'eau.*

Years later, I came upon the old, familiar student song in Jean Renoir's book about his father.

Quite another type of explanation was required by a song like

> *Connaissez-vous la rosière,*
> *La rosière de chez nous?*
> *De trois bimbims elle est mère,*
> *La rosière;*
> *Elle n'a jamais un époux,*
> *La rosière de chez nous.*

The joke was that, although *rosière* meant the village virgin, the virgin of our village was different from most, what with three little bastards.

When my father sang those songs, told those stories walking down the hill in the morning, his face lit up with laughter and his eyes sparkled. I had the strong feeling that he was poised for flight. At any moment he might take off, leave my mother and me for that life I imagined on the other side of the world. But then he would look down at me and say, "Don't you think so, old girl?" and I knew he was staying. Each time it was a fresh relief.

At the same time, I was well aware that my father would do anything I wanted. Once as we were walking along I was taken by a wild flower — a cardinal growing in a bog on the other side of the fence — and my father, in his clothes for going to town and his hard straw hat, lay down on his stomach on the tar sidewalk, reached under the fence, and got it for me.

From other stories, heard with a half of my mind that was ignorant of the jokes, I knew my father had been an exemplary son, not only to his father, but to his mother. My mother told me once with pride that, when my father went out into the world, he promised his mother he would keep himself pure for his future wife. In the same compartment as this information were stories of my father's growing up in a minister's household in Roxbury, even then turning into a slum. Nice little boys wore plaid skirts, something like kilts, till they were quite big. My father was tormented by the little tough boys of Roxbury, who used to call, "Hello, sis!" when he came out. The story was that, after years of beg-

ging his mother to let him start wearing breeches he was
finally given a pair, and in them marched proudly out into
the street, only to be met with, "Hello, sis with trousers
on!"

To believe two mutually exclusive things requires nothing
but practice. When I myself went out into the world of New
York, it seemed perfectly possible to navigate on the belief
that my father had been the life of the Left Bank, while still
accepting that he was pure as the driven snow. Both aspects
of this agreeable proposition were essential. I'd found that a
father who had studied in Paris under Lefèbre and Doucet,
who had lived the old *vie de bohème,* was a great asset in my
background. When I was in another mood, like everyone else
on earth I needed my father who was good.

I was in my twenties, married, and separated from my husband before this image began to come apart. I had a beau
whose dry wit and ironic cast of thought reminded me of
my father's. To keep my conversational end up, I used my father's jokes, in talking to Oliver. I seemed to remember everything my father ever said to me, as though I had inherited
my repartee. I also told Oliver stories about my father. He
said he wished he knew him.

One weekend my father came down to New York to pay
my year-old baby a visit. I asked Oliver to come for lunch
on Sunday. My father, who never took but the minimum
time off from painting, left Boston on the midnight train
and arrived Sunday morning. When I went to meet him,
away from the familiar environs of my visits home, it was a
terrible shock. Old, gray, stooped, he seemed so terribly
tired. I never knew *that* was how he looked. It was like one

image superimposed upon another that doesn't fit. I felt he must need fresh air, and took him for a long walk up York Avenue.

When Oliver came, the conversation was not at all what I had imagined. Nothing either of them said was especially funny. They did not spark each other to wit. They were subdued, resigned. If they were caustic, it was sadly. After we finished lunch, my baby was brought in from his nap and sat, a great, rosy, goggling peony, on his grandfather's knee. Oliver sat opposite them, smoking innumerable cigarettes.

"That's a nice baby," he said.

"A very nice baby," my father said, and to his pink grandson, "Hello, Job Lots."

The next week when I went out to dinner with Oliver I told him how sorry I was my father wasn't in good form on Sunday — I thought he'd looked exhausted. And I had so wanted him to be at his best!

"I liked him the way he was," Oliver said. "I'm a tired man myself."

But my father was not merely tired, he was dying. He lived only a week or two after that. A telegram summoning me to his bedside came in the morning, to the magazine where I worked, and I took a noon train to Boston. He was dead when I got to the hospital, from peritonitis. My mother sat in a small, private room of the hospital waiting for me, with tears pouring down her flushed cheeks.

I secured a two weeks' leave of absence to clear out my father's studio. The day after the funeral, when I let myself in by the door on the balcony, the colored elevator boy was roaming around downstairs; also a slatternly creature who for years had maintained the fiction of tidying up, though between her corns and the number of things my father didn't want disturbed, black grit from the Boston & Maine Railroad, on the other side of the vast north window, always lay on everything. When she was coming, my father used to remark, "We're getting the feminine touch today." One of his studio pupils, a talented eight-year-old, misunderstood him, and after that my father, delighted by what she thought he'd said, called the cleaning woman Old Cinnamon Touch.

She was well named. She, and the elevator boys, and the janitor, as well as several indigent painters, used to borrow money from my father with no intention, apparently, of paying it back. He could never refuse. He would come home to the country, the corner of his mouth pulled down under his mustache in a way that meant life seemed especially grim. "The way to make an enemy is to lend him money," he would say.

Now there were only those two in the studio of all the pupils and models, the other painters in the building who used to drop in, the paint salesmen insisting on showing the contents of their suitcases, who used to throng the place. I came down the stairs from the balcony. "Ah, yours is the terrible loss," Old Cinnamon Touch said, lugubriously. Soon after, she and the elevator boy went away. When I got back to New York my mother wrote me that some of the best pictures were missing, as well as quantities of paints, brushes, and drawing paper.

The studio contained the accumulation of forty years, and I had had no idea of how, properly, to go about organizing such a mess. Canvases eight or ten deep leaned against the walls. Boxes upon boxes of dusty pastels lay open on tables invisible under the load. There were stacks of *Saturday Evening Posts* running back to 1914. Boxes and trunks were crammed with rumpled costumes for models. There was dirt everywhere. It was the saddest place I have ever been in.

A place just quitted by someone beloved does not merely speak of the person. It is the person. The scent of my father's presence was in the air, and I felt in precisely the same relationship with it as I had with him. I sat in one of the small rooms off the balcony, trying to bring order into his old bank statements, unopened business letters, and the stock certificates I had found.

Beyond the door lay the great, motionless space of the two-story studio where he had worked so unceasingly. Now and then the boards of the staircase would creak, as they used to creak when he pounded up them to open the door. Motes of dust floated along a beam of sunshine from the unwashed window beside me. I took another box of papers—a small, square box—from the shelf in the closet. Even while I was sitting down again to open it, I felt a thrill of foreboding. *This is the fatal box,* something in me said. Something said, *Now I will know.* My heart beat fast—it was as if, all my life, unconsciously I had been waiting for this moment to discover the secret of my father.

Half the box was filled with a sort of release, written in my father's hand and signed by various names, some of which I recognized as those of old models. One of them said, "I hereby state that my mother is no longer in need of medical aid and I will no longer pretend that she is." All of

them said something like, "I promise not to bother Mr.
Hale for any more money. I have received full and sufficient payment for my services." Underneath these was an
erotic love poem, written in my father's hand, folded and
worn as though it had been carried in a billfold. At the bottom was a packet of letters written on beautiful gray paper
with a crest at the top and the address — Palazzo Borghese.
The Roman postmarks on the envelopes were only a year
old. "My dearest Phil," they began. "I can never tell you
what your letter means to me," one read. "Bless you for it,
and for letting me know it would mean something to you
to hear from me. Dear — good night. I feel as though we
had just come back from a walk at Giverny. Would that it
were so! After all, what were the intervening years if they
have left us practically unchanged." And another: "There
was this — that I was conscious of — a certain grim endurance
— a suppressed sadness, that wrung my heart. I may be
wrong, but happy you didn't seem to be. You are so brave,
so uncomplaining, so selfless." One letter said, "Your love
for Nancy and hers for you is enough, even if there were
nothing else in your life to put you beyond and above
pity."

When I came back to the empty, silent studio from my
contemplation of the old papers, it was as if my childhood's
equilibrium had been hopelessly shattered. The proposition
had restated itself tragically.

I have a memorial of how my father's studio looked, in a
painting of his that was lost from sight many years, found,
and then exhibited in the fiftieth anniversary re-enactment

of the famous 1913 Armory Show. My mother got a letter, one summer when I was visiting her at the house by the sea, from the director of the re-enactment, reminding her that two paintings of my father's had been in the original show — one of a group of students, he said, the other a nude. The director needed them for the repeat performance.

We didn't know what had become of either picture. By advertising in the New York *Times*, we located the group painting. My father had, characteristically, given it away — to the student who, all these years later, saw and answered the advertisement. We continued to look for the other picture. The director's description of it was "Nude in sunlit studio." My mother remembered such a composition, but I couldn't. Later that summer, in the attic where my father's unsold canvases were stacked, I came on the picture behind some old frames. I recognized it from the description, but it was so dirty and the rip in it posed such an immediate problem in restoring that I didn't get any particular reaction to it.

The following spring my mother and I attended the gala opening of the Armory Show. Ladies and gentlemen in evening dress strolled through the galleries formed by partitioning off the old building on lower Lexington Avenue, viewing the pictures that had caused such a stir in 1913. My mother's du Maurier beauty was more spectacular than ever now that her hair was snow-white. She looked like a duchess, and was — as usual in big crowds — shy, critical, and anxious to leave. When she got in this mood, funny things were apt to pop into her head. Standing with me in front of the slat-like cubes of the famous Duchamps painting, she said, "When that was first shown, it looked peculiar even to us artists. Your father wrote a limerick about it."

"What?" I said.

She recited:

> *If, returning from one of your bats,*
> *You expected pink cows and blue rats,*
> *But a lady, quite bare,*
> *Descended the stair,*
> *Now wouldn't that rattle your slats?*

"You appreciate the picture now, don't you?" I asked severely. The urge to improve one's parents never wears thin.

"Oh, I like it better than most nudes," she said airily. "All those fat, pink angleworms!"

One never ceases to insist on meticulous consistency from them, either. "You always taught *me* the nude was beautiful, and that it was benighted to think anything else," I reproached her.

"Did I?" she said.

I strolled away to look at pictures by myself.

After I had looked at my father's dark, laughing students for a bit, some paintings nearby struck me afresh with the perennial Impressionist miracle: the light of the world shattered and remade in the eye. My father's nude, just beyond, was also *pointilliste* — he was still painting in his French manner. In these public surroundings, the picture burst upon me in radiant floods of light as if I had never seen it before.

Against the great studio window Carrie stands, flourishing a gauzy scarf through which she is revealed, posed as though dancing. She is looking down at her feet; her face is hidden by a pompadour of clinging, coppery hair. Beyond the studio window, in full sunlight, rises the pink brick steeple of a church. Inside, a big pier glass of the kind painters use to view their work in reverse makes a balance to the church, in the composition. And reflected in the mirror — tiny, tiny, so that it is no wonder the director's description of the painting, based on a photograph, didn't include it — stands the figure of my father painting the picture.

Even so minutely, it shows the father I knew — his characteristic painting stance, legs apart; the white shirt-sleeves and stiff collar he always wore; the walrus mustache; the same melancholy eyes. The picture's title in the catalogue was, simply, "Nude"; but suddenly I remembered — I can't imagine from where, it must have been from earliest childhood because I hadn't even remembered the picture — that my father's old, joking name for it was "The World, the Flesh, and the Devil." It seemed like a portrait of my father.

Looking at the sad little face in that picture full of sun, I was able at last to admit to myself that my father had really not been a gay man at all, but a retiring man who assumed ebullience to cheer himself up, and to get along in a world he had no instinct to overwhelm. The things in his life he picked out to actually do, and not do, prove how he sought and clung to safety in the bosom of his tiny, adoring family. When he needed escape, he had a companion to escape with: for when I used to get the feeling, walking down the hill, that he was poised to take off for the world of my illusion, I was right; we did; on wings of recollection we flew far away. Even his failure to set the world on fire shows, in its own complicated, wry way, how my father did after all fulfill himself. He couldn't have really wanted fame on the grand scale or it would have come easier to him. In spite of all that batting his head against the wall of success, his inward nature preserved him from retaliating against his father by becoming like him. He loved the art of painting, and what he really wanted was to be at home quietly with my mother.

"Aren't you ready to go *yet?*" my mother said when I rejoined her at the far end of the gallery.

"Don't you want to go and look at Papa's pictures one more time?" I said. "I hate to go away and leave them."

"I know every picture your father ever painted by heart," she said.

Her belief was always that my father was perfect — a great, unappreciated painter. It was no surprise to her when, toward the end of the Armory Show, the nude was bought by a gentleman in the Middle West. What she said was, "It's about time somebody had a look at all that wonderful technical skill. All that training. Nobody has any training, nowadays."

I had been about to say something about her turning against nudes, and her keeping the picture up in the attic herself for thirty years; but then, suddenly, in the middle years of my life, it dawned on me I might not know about both sides of my mother's mind either.

A Good Light

AFTER my father's death, my mother could not seem to enjoy anything any more. The light had gone out of gardening, to which she had always given most of her time when she was not actually painting. When I came home from New York, where I lived in my twenties, I would point out to her the extreme folly of her lack of interest. "You mustn't let that wonderful garden you've built up run down," I said.

"But I don't take any pleasure in it!" she said. I disapproved of how piteous her large, gray eyes looked. "It makes me feel horrid when I try to work. To be doing it by myself without your father."

"But he was away all day," I pointed out. I solved her

problem by adding, "It's a mistake to live in the past."

She did not even want to paint any more. In vain did I demonstrate how unwise it was to let her great talent lie fallow.

"I hate painting now," she said. "It's somehow horrible."

"You need to make an effort," I said. "That poking around in the attic with old letters isn't worthy of you. You always told *me* art was worth more than all the other activities on earth."

She only gazed dumbly at her child who was throwing back at her, as children must, the maternal words.

In New York, I went out to dinner with a doctor beau and spent part of the evening telling him about how badly my poor mother was adjusting to the death of my father.

"Loss of libido," declared Raymond, who practiced a little light analysis on the side, nodding. "I'd be glad to discuss therapy with her if you want to send her to me."

On my mother's next visit to me I proposed Raymond.

"I don't see how it could do any good, but I'll try," she said, docile as a young girl, and as earnest. "I don't see how a doctor's going to make me feel any better about how I never really appreciated your father." Tears came into her eyes.

"Mother, dear. You *worshiped* Papa," I said. But there was no reasoning with her. "Just tell Raymond everything that's troubling you," I told her. "Psychoanalysis is a new science, and they are able to make you more objective."

"I *am* objective," she said sadly. "It's when your father was alive that I wasn't objective. How's the doctor going to alter that? It's too late."

"Just trust him," I said, full of confidence in Raymond and Freud.

So off she went into the New York streets, in her black felt sailor hat, wearing her rubbers and carrying an umbrella as if there was no such thing as a taxi.

When she got back she was tight-lipped and wouldn't discuss the appointment. She had another for later in the week.

"I'm not going back to that man," she said when she came home from that one. "*You* may like him, but I think he's just horrid."

"What's so horrid now?" I said with asperity, feeling that wariness of knowing one is going to have to take sides against one's parent.

"He was. All he wanted to talk about was . . . *sex*. It was bad enough last time, when he wanted me to tell him all sorts of things about your father that are none of his business. But today this friend of yours asked me whether I had any . . . feelings . . . about him! Whether I was attracted to him! He said I must realize it was perfectly normal if I was. I never even saw him until this week! I think he's a slimy pig."

"Oh, Mother," I said. "Raymond was only hoping you would make a good transference."

"I don't care what he was hoping," my mother said. "You could see he wasn't a gentleman."

It must have been shortly after that debacle that my mother turned to religion in an effort to assuage her grief.

The household I grew up in was nominally Unitarian. I was sent to a Unitarian Sunday school (where in those days they taught Bible stories like any other Sunday school, in-

stead of growing seeds to study the Life Force). Once in a
long while — I can't remember what occasioned it — my
mother and father went to church, with me walking between them down the hill. We sat in the square pew of the
white Colonial edifice, and afterward walked home to Sunday dinner.

At the table my father would begin by giving an imitation of Mr. Parker preaching the sermon, and work up to
stories of the pranks he and his brothers used to play in his father's church. In the hymnbook they used there was a
footnote to the familiar hymn "All Hail the Power of Jesus'
Name." The little Hale boys used to sing the footnote instead of the hymn — it fitted the music perfectly:

> *This tune was a great favorite*
> *Of the late President Dwight.*
> *It was often sung in the co-o-ollege choir*
> *When he, catching, as it were,*
> *The inspiration of the hour,*
> *Would join — the — heav'nly chor-i-us!*

My father used also to render the boys' scurrilous imitation
of their father and their sister Nelly, responsively reading as
they never had a psalm that never was:

"Slew the Ephesians!" boomed out the great, deep voice.

"For his mercy endureth forever," piped the little voice.

"Og, King of Bashan."

"For his mercy endureth forever."

"Chopped all their heads off!"

"For his mercy endureth forever."

"Sawed all their legs off!"

"For his mercy endureth forever."

My mother was brought up Congregational — a sort of alleviation her own mother made of the hellfire Presbyterianism of her preacher father, who had been a missionary to Chicago when its streets were mud. But when my mother married my father she embraced the Unitarian church just as she embraced everything else about the Hales, whom she held to be perfection. (That her embrace was never too tight for comfort is proved by a story she told me — that my Grandfather Hale himself said, shortly after her marriage, "Lily, don't get into church work, whatever you do. You won't be able to get any painting done.")

Now when I went home I was embarrassed by my mother's little volumes of devotions — some of them very old, since she was far too economical to spend money on a brand-new devotional book when the house was full of ones dating from my grandfather's day. She used to read them during her very early breakfasts — alone, because I got up late. *Helps by the Way* — that was the type of title. I opened *Helps* once, to the following verse:

> *"So!"— by small, slow footsteps,*
> *By the daily cross,*
> *By the heart's unspoken yearning,*
> *By its grief and loss;*
> *So, He brings them home to rest,*
> *With the victors, crowned and blessed.*

I shut the book again hastily, blushing at my mother's taste in consolation. What she needed was to have a good time, I thought; enjoy herself. But my mother had always had such incomprehensible ways of enjoying herself.

She tried going to the Unitarian church, but she said it

didn't satisfy her somehow. Her way of putting it was that she wasn't intellectual enough to appreciate Unitarianism. In the years since I went to Sunday school, the church had become highly humanistic. "There isn't anything to look *at*," my mother said. "No cross or anything."

I told her, and her Episcopalian sister told her, that since she found the Unitarian church empty, she ought to look somewhere else. She went to stone-Gothic St. Paul's a few times, but that didn't satisfy her, either. "I hate just sitting there like a great bump while everybody else goes up to the altar," she said.

"Then why not go up too?" I said. "After all, you were christened. I read that the Archbishop of Canterbury says anybody baptized in the name of the Father and the Son and the Holy Ghost can take Communion."

My mother's face lit up, as it always did when something reminded her of my father. "Do you remember that christening story your father used to tell about your grandfather?" she said. "The old gentleman was getting deaf by that time, and the baby's mother had a lisp. 'What's the name of this child?' he said. Even when he whispered his voice was enormous. 'Luthy, thir,' the mother said. 'Lucifer? Nonsense!' your grandfather rumbled. 'John, I baptize thee . . .' And that, your father said, is how Lucy Perkins came to be christened John."

Next time I saw my mother I asked if she had gone up to the rail yet.

"I went once," she said. "But I can't keep on doing that. I'm not a member! I don't feel as if they really wanted me."

"Then join the church, for pity's sake," I said.

"Oh, no. I couldn't possibly," she said. "All the Hales were Unitarians. It would be disloyal to them." She looked as dutiful and good as a young girl.

But she also looked lumpy, in those days. Her figure had got out of hand, and she had backaches. She started going to an orthopedist in Boston. The next time I came up for a visit she was deep in the mystique of posture exercises.

"He says the seat of the soul is right here," she said, laying her hand on her solar plexus.

She would sit only on straight chairs — erect but easy, as she was being taught to do. Her gaze tended to look inward, like a Hindu's. She had even acquired missionary fervor, and made me consult the orthopedist, too. My experience with him was hardly more successful than hers with Raymond. When the doctor bounced lightly up and down on his toes and said, "Look at me! This is perfect posture!" he received less than my full approbation. "How *can* you think so highly of that man, after once knowing Papa?" I said.

When my father died, his sister Nelly presented my mother with a house on Cape Ann. It had been my grandfather's custom to give each of his sons a house when they married, but when my parents married they didn't want a house. They were going to live in their studio, and I was not to be so much as thought of for another six years. Aunt Nelly's gift represented the house my father never got.

After mother began going there in the summer, her gardening instincts revived. What woke her interest was the appearance in her life of organic gardening. Now, when I came up for visits there, I found Mr. Rodale a sacred name around the house. There was also, I learned, a high priestess in England named Lady Eve Balfour, who ran an experimental farm for raising crops organically.

Making and augmenting an enormous compost heap became as much a ritual in my mother's life as her posture exercises. With great trouble and infinite effort she used to bury all our garbage; it would then be dug up by dogs and the raccoon who haunted the grounds of nights; then my mother would bury it again. The world was full of sin — people not only used commercial fertilizer but failed to use the organic when it lay right at hand. Look at Disposalls! With her early breakfasts, my mother took to reading a magazine called *The Soil.* The Devil's name was Chemicals.

"But, Mother," I would say, restraining myself. "Everything in the world is made of chemicals, one way or another."

"You mean natural chemicals," she retorted.

"A chemical's a chemical, dear. They make things out of chemicals in the laboratory."

"Synthetically!" she hissed.

The reason there are in the stone house by the sea, to this day, five one-pound cans of cocoa is that my mother, who loved a good cup of hot chocolate, couldn't find a brand that did not violate her principles, and was, of course, too economical to throw away even one that did. In the ingredients listed on the labels, one can confesses to containing not chocolate but "delicious chocolate flavor." Two other brands both say, "Artificially flavored with vanillin." There are two cans of a fourth brand, but even the newer of them, purchased after an interval during which my mother hoped the manufacturer might have repented, says, "Chocolate flavor."

It was a great relief to me when she started painting again. There was no question but what, after the interim, her work was better than ever. Something had pulled it together. Forceful black accents pointed up what had always been her exquisitely sensitive charcoal technique. Her painting in oil had become looser, more *dégagé*. She had always had a command of line; but now to see her holding a brush — she used very small camel's-hair brushes — at arm's length, eyes intent on what she was painting, and then make an acute, intricate, nervous line down the canvas made you know that somehow behind the scenes she had moved; as was said of Renoir, she had changed from a worshiper of nature to one able to dominate it. It was very mysterious. My mother was as girlish, as frequently absurd, as ever; but when she was painting you would not dream of teasing her. She was like a ship moving majestically under full sail.

"I'm glad to see you getting so much done," I said one morning. We were in the studio by the sea, built by my aunt to include what used to be considered the ideal adjunct to painting — an alcove back of the great studio window so the painter can get behind his light. "Don't you feel this represents true devotion for you? I mean, artists are supposed to find their religion in painting."

My mother could look blanker than anybody. "I don't know what you mean," she said, poking delicately at the rose madder on her palette with the tip of her brush.

"Don't you feel you sort of fulfill yourself, in art?" I said.

"I try to be a good painter," she said. Her gaze shifted to

the canvas, and with that curious encompassing stare of an artist she deposited the speck of paint in a precise spot.

I tried once more. "You don't seem to feel you have to fool with churches any more."

"What's church got to do with it?" Her eyes went back to her palette.

I must have stirred up some reaction, though not the one I intended, for at dinner she said, "The only thing your father ever did that doesn't seem entirely kind and understanding was the way he used to make fun of church. *He* was a great intellectual, and I know he was *deeply* religious. But he *might* have left a little of church standing for me!"

It was the first time, at least since his death, I ever heard her criticize my father, and I don't know but what it was the last. Until her own death my mother continued to praise my father as though he had just died and her mind was still filled with his perfections. After her death I began to appreciate how she'd felt.

When someone beloved dies, one dies too. At least that is what it feels like, or, rather, one imagines it feels like. The sensations are well known in literature. There is the loss of color from one's surroundings, the sensation of emptiness, the sense of loss of connection. One knows perfectly well what's the matter, at the same time struggling, as though in deep water, for a fingerhold on something — anything — to pull one back to life.

All my friends reminded me that time is the great healer. Marian, a neighbor, turned back at the door after her call, to make a concrete suggestion. "You mustn't allow yourself to live in the past," she said. "Perform an *operation* on the past. When my mother died, I just took all her clothes out into the yard behind her house and burned them."

I considered it. But later when I came to pick up my mother's old beige cardigan sweater, it *was* kindness, and her matter-of-fact embrace. When I looked at the little gray cotton suit she wore to Italy just before she died, it *was* the posture she achieved over the years, so pretty and erect. I didn't mind the idea of burning up clothes, I told Marian when I saw her, but I couldn't bear to burn the love residing in them.

"That's silly," she said. "Your mother isn't in material things."

I tried doing posture exercises, for there no longer seemed anything so horrendous about doing them. Except that I could find no pleasure in it. Perhaps remembering my mother's regrets about church, I tried going back to the Unitarians.

I found it worried me, too, that there was no object on which to fix my trapped and struggling contemplation. "Why doesn't the church have a cross any more? They used to have a cross, when I was a child," I said to the minister at the door one Sunday after service.

"A cross is a symbol," the minister said — a handsome man, youthful and bouncy on his toes, with curly, graying hair.

I looked out toward the sunshine beyond the church porch. "What's the matter with a symbol?" I said.

"You want to look out for symbols. They're freighted," he said.

I tried the Episcopal church, where they did have a cross I could contemplate. The rector, a tall man with a face full of exaltation and pain, like Lincoln's, preached a simple, feeling sermon. One afternoon I asked him and his wife to come for a drink. When they were saying goodbye, the rector's wife said, "What beautiful things you have in your house!"

"They all came from my mother," I said.

The rector must have been trying to console me. "I never knew the meaning of spiritual freedom," he said, "until I realized one day I could truly say that I didn't care whether my house and all its contents burned down or not."

"He's talking about material things," his wife said hastily.

After my mother's death I began to see her as she had really been. Now that all occasion for disagreement was gone, the resulting chasm seemed filled by a tide of praise — objective, discerning. It was less like losing someone than discovering someone. I could see my mother's face as it had looked a hundred times: earnest, gentle, misinformed, good. What was there but loveliness in all that? I saw her in her little black rubbers and black sailor hat, paddling along with a serious expression, carrying her umbrella just in case.

When I cooked dinner she would never again come up behind me and switch the electric burner off high to save electricity. The trick always enraged me, but now I saw why she'd had to do it. Like all real artists', her objective had been to create riches with modest means; squandering seemed to her a kind of stupidity. Since she never had but one standard, perfection — which in the nature of things fits art better than life — she often gave a misleading impression of Yankee parsimony. But she would really only be trying to make a dish of, say, creamed potatoes the way she would make a drawing — consummately, with an economy of means.

Was it remorse I felt? I wondered, putting away after-dinner coffee cups one afternoon in my house in Virginia. After all, I had done all the appreciating of my mother I was capable of, while she was alive; I just hadn't been objective. I put another of the little coffee cups up on the kitchen shelf. My mother had given them to me. I felt a pang as I visualized her receiving them as a wedding present — young, with her lovely life before her. It gave me a sort of nausea to remember how briskly I had recommended panaceas after my father died and she would say, her eyes pleading for sympathy, that she felt horrid. *Make an effort. . . . Don't let things slip, or nature will take over. . . .* How right I was! When the world loses color, gray jungle encroaches more and more on the clearing you are in. The thought came to me that what I felt was not so much remorse, not grief, as it was desire, for what I had not been able to stand apart from my mother enough to do: just purely enjoy her.

The idea was so new to me that all I could do was stand perfectly still. My coffee cups are bowl-shaped, with narrow, bright-green rims, and little bunches of Dresden flowers. They were among the china that used to be in the cabinet in the dining room of our house in Dedham; as a child I would stand with my hands behind my back, staring at its wonders. It was probably not right that moment in my Virginia kitchen, but memory makes it seem suddenly, that the cup in my hand, before my eyes, looked wonderful once more, its color vibrant, like a tiny painted shallop come sailing in with tidings of comfort and joy.

So, by each cup and saucer . . . In my living room, on an

end table, is a vase, strong blue, with a gilt rim and a picture of an eighteenth-century lady with a long curl, that
also used to be in that china cabinet. I don't know its origin;
history seems to be unnecessary for putting the animation in
inanimate objects. The vase always gave me a special feeling, and now it gives me a special feeling again — a feeling
carried over, like freight. My mother used to call that kind
of delight a "feel." I have a feel for some pale-green glass finger bowls, on a shelf in the storeroom, that I have no real
use for, but that I wouldn't dream of throwing away, any
more than I would a message from the past. When I look at
them I almost shiver — their green is opalescent, their glass
a mere film; they are like great bubbles blown out of green
soap.

I said something of these pleasures to Marian one day
when she came to tea. She said, "I didn't realize you were a
china and crystal collector."

"I'm not exactly," I began, and giggled. I hope she didn't
think I was laughing at anything she said. I was only remembering a story of my mother's about how indignant she
was, as a desperately ambitious art student, when a society
lady said, "Miss Westcott! Do you aspire to china painting?"
If I told Marian I was collecting feelings she would say it
was silly. The Unitarian minister might say they carried too
much freight, and the rector might think they weren't spiritual enough. But at least I could enjoy them.

At first when I went to the stone house by the sea, it felt
both empty and crowded with the objective reality of my
mother that I had overlooked. Her absence seemed abysmal.
Later in the summer, when the season had turned — the

time of year when the Dipper tips up as though ceasing to spill honey into our cove, and you can smell the ripening apples of autumn — I went down to the rocks where we swim. Lying on my stomach in my bathing suit, arms folded under my chin, I looked at the pink granite two inches before my eyes, where some infinitesimal red spiders ran. Then I turned over on my side and looked at the loosestrife growing in a deep crevice between the rocks. I didn't know much about wild flowers, but all at once I could see, as I certainly never saw before, how beautiful these particular ones were. They had long spires, off which burst purple blossoms — but to say purple is not enough; they were radiant, orchid-tinged; like jewels in that afternoon light.

"Do you know what family loosestrife belongs to?" I asked a little boy sunning himself.

"No. Can you do botany?" he said with interest.

"No," I said, concluding the conversation. For when you catch anything looking as beautiful as that, you had better keep perfectly still and enjoy it, hoping it doesn't change.

The loosestrife did change. Each spire began to look like a mace, a scepter; and the blossoms up its length like purple gems — adamantine, sharp. But I found that by blinking my eyes I could make it go back to being a flower again. After all, that is what it was — a flower, and beautiful. The scepter was only a fancy.

The Other Side

AFTER my mother died, while I was still in the condition of love and appreciation of her quality that for a long time washed over me like a sea, among other tasks I felt I should go through such of my mother's drawings as were in Virginia; there had been inquiries from would-be purchasers, and I needed to see which, if any, I felt ready to part with. In addition to drawings glassed and framed, with cards from old exhibitions still pasted to the backing, there were big black French portfolios full of drawings, some of which I hadn't seen for years and years, many only partly finished. As I drew out each sheet of Strathmore board, propped it against a chair, and viewed it, all the pictures seemed to have taken on a curious new dimension that at first baffled me.

Here was the shed behind our house in Dedham. Tortuous black branches on which a few black berries cling are shown in relation to its slanting, white-laden roof, the whole vignetted on the white paper so that the scene seems drowned in winter. Here was the house across the road seen from the windows of our upstairs hall. Upon the boughs of the hemlock on the front lawn, bent down by snow, snow is still falling; but inside the window, in the foreground, blossoms of a bowl of freesias are touched faintly with sanguine chalk, giving a sense at once of inwardness and of warmth. Next came the profile of a little Irish girl my mother used often as a model: tiptilted, naïve, sharp black against the strong light from the window where she is sitting.

What seemed so new? Looking at the old, familiar scenes and faces made me long for something, but it wasn't the past. It was something here in the pictures themselves. What I was discovering, throughout the long series of drawings, was a likeness: a self-portrait that my mother had not the least awareness she was making.

My father used to tell the story that when the alienist Weir Mitchell went to an exhibition of Sargent's paintings, he stood for a long time in front of a portrait of one of his old patients, and then said, "Now I can see what was the matter with him." The unconscious revelation about herself that I began to take in as I viewed my mother's drawings right after her death seemed almost as eerie, and had to do with the choice of subjects — those little girls, like flowers; those interiors, snug, sheltering, unpeopled; and everywhere those repeatedly pictured, exquisite falls of snow. It was all true, especially the snow.

Coldness was puzzling, coming from that tall, beautiful, glowing creature who enchanted all who met her in warm moods. She was a loving mother, an adoring wife, yet all my life (since the days when I would sit in her lap in the bathroom in a white painted chair, very sturdy, that was all the jungle gym I ever needed, for her to brush my hair) I had known the change that could take place in her and, as a child, I would be stricken with fear. It was as if she had gone away and forgotten me. She wasn't merely thinking about something else; she had ceased to feel my presence. What had I done? Did she not love me any more?

After I grew up I used to talk it over with my Aunt Nancy, whose spirits — high unlike my mother's — were undimmed by her health — poor unlike my mother's. My mother's coldness distressed us in just the same way. To nobody else would we have admitted she possessed a single flaw, but there it was. We hated it when all outsiders saw of her was the ramrod back, the absence of maternal softness, the lack of feminine susceptibility to masculine presence. She herself never would admit she was cold. "No I'm not!" she'd protest. "I was being very cordial!" Her reproachful eyes made you hate yourself for blurting out that you thought she was. Once in a while my aunt and I sought each other's sympathy for wounds of our own that my mother didn't even know she had inflicted.

There was the time I had been ill at a sanatorium for over a year, and at last telephoned to say I would be able to come home the following weekend. My mother — who had written me almost daily, who made my sanatorium Christmas merry with a dozen presents wrapped, inimitably, in white paper with green plaid taffeta ribbons — said, "I'm sorry, you will have to come later. I have a cold." My aunt could sympathize; she knew those colds of my mother's — how immutable they were, how she retired to bed at their inception and remained there till free of the least sniffle. Once, while I was on a trip and moving about so rapidly I received no mail, at last about nine one evening I called up on the telephone from an inn. My son, who was visiting his grandmother, answered. We talked a bit and then I asked to speak to her. My son returned, reporting, "She's gone to bed and says she can't come to the telephone." It seemed incomprehensible, even though I remembered how rigid my mother's bedtime had always been. In the days when my father used to read to her after supper, she would rise in the middle of a chapter, announcing with an only half-mocking, theatrical intensity, "It's *ten o'clock!*"

Not only could I not have sent her message, I couldn't imagine how anybody could send it. "I know," my aunt said. "Lily's always been that way, even when she was little. Your grandmother was deeply hurt when she asked Lily whom she loved best and Lily said Annie Langer. . . . Of course the reason for *that*," Aunt Nancy said, hastening as ever to absolve her sister of blame, "was that your grandmother was utterly prostrated during the years Lily was little, so it fell to Annie to take the care of her. Lily was actually the most sensitive of us all."

I knew, however, that it was not just during those years; all my life I'd heard my tiny, sharp-tongued Grandmother Westcott exclaim, "I am utterly prostrated!" Along with that word "prostrated," "sensitive" and "resigned"—"We

must be resigned"— were words I associated with her and resented. For one thing, I didn't believe it; sometimes I felt
the whole Westcott story had been invented just so everybody — so sensitive — could be prostrated and resigned.
Yet I had also been told how, after my grandfather died leaving no money, it was my grandmother who kept things
going by taking in boarders and giving piano lessons. Such
was her fortitude that, even in straitened circumstances, she
never wavered in her determination to give her two talented daughters the best training, one in the violin, the
other in painting. It was paradoxical, but also bleak to a degree; penny-pinching New England at its starkest. I shunned
that side of my inheritance. Like my mother, who was not
one to talk about prostration or resignation, I tended to con-
centrate on the slightly bohemian Hales — a family once
known in Boston as the Dirty Delightfuls, and who were,
furthermore, famous.

I knew the general outlines of the story, laid in Victorian
Hartford. Mr. Westcott — that was how my grandmother referred to her husband to the day of her death at eighty-
seven — had something to do with guns; he went on trips
concerned with the sale of gunsights — or was it patents on
gunsights? There once were three little girls — pretty as flowers in old yellowing photographs — but the oldest, called
Dolly, died of a ruptured appendix at the age of nine while
away in Winsted visiting her Auntie Gilbert. The family
never forgot Dolly. Sayings of hers, half a century after her
death, were among the little-girl stories I did enjoy hearing.
It was she who said, with pride, "Papa spanked me, and
now I'm *all good!*" That was the kind of Victorian little girls

they were. Then there was the story of my mother and the chocolate mouse. When she was about six, for a special reward her mother gave her a penny to go and buy herself a chocolate mouse at the store on Asylum Avenue. But tragedy struck. A big rough boy laughed at Lily's fat brown curls bouncing as she trotted along, and gave her a push. She fell into a puddle, got her dress all muddy, and the penny slid through a crack in the sidewalk. Lost forever! Lily arrived back at the house on Sigourney Street dissolved in tears, because now never, never would she have that chocolate mouse. The story ended happily, for Annie Langer changed her dress, and her mother said, "Here is another penny, dear." Such bounty had never been envisioned by the infant mind. Off trotted Lily, fresh and clean once more, and able at the last to enjoy her chocolate mouse.

Happy endings were rare at Sigourney Street. My grandmother, daughter of a hellfire-preaching Presbyterian minister, had been, as far back as the Hornell, New York, Female Seminary from which she was graduated, delicate. Childbirths utterly prostrated her, and there was always her back — so painful that the doctor sometimes applied red-hot irons as a counterirritant. For all she pattered about our house briskly on little satin-slippered feet, she used to say that if she were to do what she really wanted to she would never get out of bed at all.

Mr. Westcott, too, was increasingly ill. I was never sure what he was increasingly ill *with*. (In my psychoanalytical phase I put it down to being married to my grandmother.) Sometimes he was said to have had inflammatory rheumatism; sometimes it was gout. He sustained, they told me, frightful attacks of asthma. His two daughters used to roll special medicated cigarettes to relieve his breathing. He struggled to keep up with his business affairs, but, along with his health, they continued to disintegrate. Business associates proved untrustworthy. The patent on one of his gunsights was stolen by a foreign government — or was it one of the business associates who stole it? It was most confused and confusing, and did not pique my curiosity in the least. I was tired of hearing my grandmother say that my grandfather died in great suffering, a disappointed man. "Suffering" was another of the words I resented, especially because I could see how the mention of suffering made my father suffer.

To my grandmother, it appeared high praise. "So-and-so is a great sufferer," she would announce approvingly, and even my mother looked respectful. While I was a child tales of the deviltries of the little Hale boys came as a great relief, and when I grew up it was a great relief to get married and go to New York to live my own life among people who had no more use for mournfulness than my father and I; and furthermore took a normal view of sex. My grandmother's views on that subject were summed up in what she used to exclaim of anybody with more than three children — "Her husband must be a beast!"

The long fingers of her abhorrence reached even into my own destiny. I had always known my father did not care for his mother-in-law — it was typical of his private sense of humor that by calling her "Dear lady," which pleased her, he could satisfy his hostility. But not until my grandmother had been dead for thirty years did my mother — the year before she died — tell me a story that explained why he, who always indulged me, never granted my life's wish for brothers and sisters.

My mother's apartment in Virginia was equipped with a curious, built-in table that partly bridged the doorway to the kitchen, and there we used to sit, drinking our tea, I slouched in my chair and she sitting straight as an arrow, at eighty-two. On the kitchen door itself she used to pin up things that pleased her eye — a bunch of seedpods, a painted Buddha suspended by a wire, clippings from the newspaper. That day it was a photograph, from the cover of the *Times Book Review,* of a naïve medieval wooden madonna holding a baby not much younger than herself.

"I love the Virgin Mother to be a child too," my mother said. "It seems so much more appropriate."

"Not to me," I said. "Motherhood ought to be big and warm and motherly."

"Oh, no," she said impatiently. "— Did I ever tell you that your grandmother never wanted your aunt and me to have children at all?"

"No!" I exclaimed.

The reason my grandmother felt that way was that she couldn't bear to have her daughters endure the ordeal that, for her, childbirth had been. Incredibly enough, she was able to effect her will. My aunt never did bear a child and, "It never occurred to me in those days that I *could* disobey my *mother,*" my own mother said. After she and my father had been married several years, however, my grandmother took Aunt Nancy to Brussels for a winter to study the violin. My father said to my mother, "Let's have a baby,

quick, before she gets back," and that was how I was born
and thought of.

The summer after my mother died and I drove alone
from Virginia to our Cape Ann house by the sea, far more
awaited me than had been required by the clearing out of
her little winter apartment. It all seemed, that first summer,
overwhelming. I could only putter about, picking up a cigar box full of squeezed-dry paint tubes and setting it down
again; hanging up a set palette — as like my mother as a photograph — from a nail on the wall as though it were her
shield. I had the feeling I could not yet bear to part with anything of hers, as though I had a mysterious need for it, now
I had no mother.

I did, however, get rid of things that belonged to other
people. There was the black leather trunk full of Hale letters my mother had always intended to read through. I'd realized all along that neither she nor I was equipped for such
a task, and now I offered them to a college library with an interest in the family. As the curator was carrying out cartons
into which she had transferred the letters, I remembered to
call her attention to a letter file I'd found lying in a corner,
on top of an album of thin-paper copies of letters. "These
seem to have belonged to my mother's father," I said. "He
had something to do with guns. Would you like them?"

The curator leafed through some letters, as I looked over
her shoulder. Those received bore ornate Victorian letter-
heads, and typically began, "My Dear Mr. Westcott, Your
favor of the 13th inst. rec'd. . . ." One of the copies of letters sent began, "I enclose herewith notes on English

translation of French translation of German experts' report Lee vs. Manson Rothwell. . . ."

"Thank you, I don't believe so," the curator replied. "It appears to be just a business file."

"I thought so, too," I said. But I couldn't bear to destroy the collection of Westcott letters.

The following summer I began turning the studio into a living room — in spite of the mocking things my parents used to say about the kind of people who, although not artists, live in "studios." The confusion was such that I decided the best way to begin was by adding to it with an immense sofa I bought at a furniture sale. I was right; once the sofa was in place it became obvious that the model stand made a good coffee table to set in front of it, and that chairs, loaded down under back issues of *Art News* and old bulletins of various museums, could be put here, and here. With this focus I could start throwing out things like the seed packets my mother collected. I gave away rolls of unused canvas, stretcher pieces, unused tubes of paint, brushes, palette knives, to a local art association.

In the course of this I came on the Westcott file box and letter book again. Before carrying them out to put in one of my three big trash cans, I lay down on the new sofa to take a breather and a look at the letters. I had not read through three before I knew I had moved into trouble — deep trouble; old unsolved trouble that sent off, from the slanting handwriting, the antiquated typing, intimations of anguish. I could not stop reading.

The letters covered not quite two years, leading up to my grandfather's death. Those that came were couched in bru-

tally inexpressive businessese, but they partook of the same
quality of horror that pervaded the replies, most of them copied in my grandmother's or my aunt's hand. It came back to
me that another of those words I used to mind so was "horrors"; "I had the horrors last night," my grandmother used
sometimes to say at breakfast. These letters had the quality
of nightmare.

Trying to figure out from the letters events only touched
on by their authors, I learned that my grandfather was Secretary and Treasurer in Hartford for the Lee Arms Company
of New York. A man named Warren, lawyer for the firm,
seems to have been one of the villains. What was it he did,
in England, with those patents? "Aside from the settlement
with Mr. Lee, practically nothing has been done," my grandfather accuses him, "while the necessity of its being attended
to is as great as it ever was. Those patents are worthless to
the company, unless they can be made productive. It was
for this you went to Europe, and *this alone*. If there be, as I
don't at all believe, really anyone in this London scheme
able and willing to carry out . . ." Mr. Warren retorts, "I
think it but fair to call attention to some of the caustic remarks that you make in your correspondence, that at times
affect a man whose skin is not as thick as a rhinoceros . . ."
and Mr. Russell, president of the company, writes to my
grandfather, "I question the wisdom of saying very much to
Mr. Warren. . . . It is very desirable not to irritate him at present, as you know how dependent we are upon him."

What was happening on the Continent? A letter from my
grandfather to Mr. Russell says, "The whole business is a
farce, and only confirms my opinion of the management of

all this German and Belgian litigation at the hands of this Mr. George Allen. This case was decided against us in May, involving hundreds of thousands of dollars. The matter was totally neglected by our representative until quite recently, and now he is expending large sums to get the case postponed for 3 months . . . wants 40 pounds to reimburse himself for traveling expenses only. I am convinced that if the company's affairs in London and Europe cannot be more carefully and judicially managed than at present the proceedings in Germany and Belgium should be promptly and forever stopped." Three months before the end, up pops a new character named Brown, in New York, who says, "Please call off your expensive lawyer and we will see what can be done. I may be able to take the matter over to Europe when I go on Bond business; and with my introductions I may get that million for you yet." Brown's letter ends, "Love to the doves," so he must have been to the house on Sigourney Street.

Who was the Mr. Winchester that, my grandfather says, months before he died, "owned the patents when I took his place in '93. These inventions, made by Pankhurst and other inventors, came from suggestions to them from me when we were having model guns made — when most of my time was spent in following up the work at Pratt and Whitney. . . . Pardon this hasty letter. I took cold in New York, came home with a chill and went to bed, and haven't been out of my room. . . . The stock sale at $54 does not, I think, indicate actual value." There are letters like one from a widow with six children who writes my grandfather, "I concluded to sell the 'Lee Arms Co.''s stock. It seemed like a *venture* to keep it, and I felt my means were not sufficient to run the risk, although it was hard for me to lose half of what was originally paid in. Now I wish to express my *thanks,* for your kindness in the matter, and for not retaining the commission. I will never forget it of you."

One of the last letters is from my grandmother herself to a Colonel Jocelyn. (Who was Colonel Jocelyn?) "After seeing you last Tuesday, Mr. Westcott went immediately to New York, but the delay of a week or ten days resulted in his failure to find Mr. McEwen." (Who was *he?*) "He had been in New York, but had left two or three days before, and it was impossible to find his address. *Probably* he was in Chicago. Mr. Westcott was greatly disappointed but returned. Friday he was taken violently ill and has been in bed suffering ever since. This *miserable* business is fast killing him. I trust you are giving his affairs your earnest attention. Their importance to us is vital." Since this letter is dated December 26th, my grandmother adds, "With the best wishes of the season"; but on January 6th a scribbled note, with my grandmother's name at the end, but copied by my aunt, is addressed to the Cashier of the Adams Express Company. "Dear Sir: I have the sad duty of informing you of the death of my husband . . . and calling your attention to his insurance policy in the Expressman's Mutual Benefit Association. I am not sure of being right in addressing this communication to you but if I am not, I entrust it to you to give notice to the proper authorities with the request that they will as soon as possible take the necessary steps to put me in possession of the amount of the policy. . . ."

When it was too depressing to read among the letters any

more I set the box and file down on the floor and lay back. I thought I could understand why they had been saved, though never referred to, all those years by my grandmother and my aunt and my mother: because they held the record — the proof — of the complicated, unendurable, never-to-be-expressed events that somehow broke them; cast over them the mysterious Victorian spell that as a child I sensed and resented. Now, with my father no longer here to protect me, I felt under the spell, too; it had only been necessary to read the letters to fall into it. More real anguish was in them than in all the rest of the more literary family letters put together. . . . And so the three women who survived were arrested, at that confluence of their emotions, like ladies in waiting at the court of the Sleeping Beauty.

When I made my appearance on the scene a few years later, they were still standing there. My grandmother, eyes cast upwards, was transfixed in her widow's attitude of nightmare woe; my aunt's pretty face bravely set, looking on the bright side. The great reversing wheel of fate was closing in on her, however, dragging her back with illnesses; the ball of one hip was to crumble away from its socket with something called osteoporosis. After a while she gave up the violin entirely. Only my mother managed, in the end, to escape. Although the subjects for pictures she painted when I was little could be called sentimental — ladies in lacy tea gowns bending over bowls of narcissi — and she, too, in those days, was always exhausted, she began, not exactly to awake, like the Sleeping Beauty, but to stir; to change her position. After my father was dead her health became excellent and her art freer.

I got up off the sofa and went to look through some drawings of hers that had been kept up here at the studio in big black wooden racks intended for etchings, to see if there was any clue there to how she — "the most sensitive of us all" — had ever done it. The first I looked at, a start on a drawing of an abandoned church far back in wintry countryside, was made in the days, shortly after my father died, when my mother was experimenting with working from her car. Perhaps the reason it was unfinished was that she got too cold for comfort. The church stands up in its graveyard small and bleak; two rows of black windows are ranged in it neat as pins, and the steeple is sharp as a needle under the merciful, falling snow. Next, another snow drawing — a della Robbia fruit-trimmed Christmas wreath, heavy with snow, hanging on a door. The next drawing was the charcoal study for a painting called "Boy by the Sea." It is of one of those *chétif*, very young children my mother saw as nobody else could: small, naked back sitting up straight on the edge of the rocking chair, one still baby hand holding the cord of a window blind, the back of the neck little and vulnerable. Even in profile the mouth is visibly set in lines of recalcitrance.

Looking at the likeness of the boy, my depression seemed to burst and release a shower of other paradoxes that supported my mother in her balancing act through life. In the core of anguish, ice. Out of ice, art — starting up again like perpetually blooming roses from an old, winter grave. The private, interior world my mother hid was at the same time just what, in her pictures, she set forth for display. The reason why she kept on developing was that she could accommodate herself to refusal to grow; but how, remains a mystery.

Say not of Beauty she is good. . . . I also understood, suddenly, about all those intransigent colds that my mother coddled, even after she was strong and healthy, as though it had been some delicate little girl she tended; those early bedtimes from which neither love nor duty could budge her. There'd been no real call to let myself be wounded by them. They were only fancies that didn't succeed — as with art — in becoming truth, self-recognitions that didn't come off. *Enshrine her and she dies, who had / The hard heart of a child.* Coldness was not a moral question in my mother, neither good nor bad. It was more the basis for survival.

Journeys

WHEN I woke the morning after we arrived in Venice, in the *pensione* room my mother and I shared, I lay still at first looking up at the arrangement of airy glass flowers, each a different color, which made the chandelier. The long, solid shutters to the French windows giving on the narrow balcony were closed, but through them strips of sunshine sifted, quivering across the ceiling in waves reflected off the little canal below. I thought about turning to the other bed to ask my mother how she was feeling.

I knew she would be exhausted after the long train trip from Genoa. There'd not even been a dining car. When the train stopped at Milan we hung out of the compartment window — the Italian-speaking friend with whom we were traveling and I — to buy fruit and pieces of chocolate which we shared three ways on the compartment table, cutting them up with a Victorian silver folding fruit knife my mother produced from her handbag. Her own mother, she said — my Grandmother Westcott — had used it in the last century, when she was traveling about Europe with her husband, trying to interest foreign governments in gunsights he had invented.

When we reached Venice it was late evening. It felt entirely unbelievable to walk out on the standard railroad station plaza, and be confronted, not with a street at all, but that stretch of black velvet water. Somehow our piles of luggage were fitted into the rocking bow of a gondola — frail, a mere shell — and we set out for the *pensione* through narrow canals, under arched bridges, around bends totally obscured by the dark of night. The Grand Canal shone with late lights when we entered it, but it too was dark and oily, wide and deep. My mother looked fearless, sitting up so straight on the oilcloth seat of the gondola. People who did not know her well — like our traveling companion — never suspected what depths of fatigue that posture of hers could conceal, what exhaustion. Such a long day's journey. . . .

. . . As when we used to go in August, my mother and I, to visit my aunt and uncle. We went on the train, in the day coach, and left my father to fend for himself. For he never would go away; would never leave his painting. . . . "Art first, life afterward," he said. Nobody ever contradicted him; my mother admired extravagantly the brilliance of his mind, and as for me, if my father said something, that meant it was so.

All the same it always seemed . . . just at first . . . a delightful escape to go away from a home I was beginning to realize was different from other children's, to the entirely ordinary household, outside New York, of my mother's sister Nancy, her doctor husband, and her new, adopted baby. The windows stood open on the burning landscape the train rattled through, and cinders got in our eyes as we ate sandwiches — deviled ham, chopped egg — that my mother had packed in a shoe box along with fruit; but it was some other knife we used to cut the fruit up with. . . . I used to eye the door to the dining car with longing. I had seen people already sitting at its white tables set with silver, being waited on by Negroes in white coats, when we walked along the South Station platform to board the train. But we were poor, and artists; besides, my mother said, dining-car food was inferior. At New Haven a man passed through the train with a flat box of provisions suspended by straps around his neck.

"Ham, chick'n ice cream," he called. "Ham, chick'n ice cream!" We bought two little cardboard boxes of ice cream striped brown, white and pink, with a round lump of orange ice. I ate all around this core, and then it was infinitely the crispest, the coldest, the best.

In late afternoon we got on another train at Grand Central, and went bucketing out over elevated tracks past tenement windows from which stared pale, hot faces with exhausted eyes. We got out onto a platform, also elevated, and descended to the street to invest in a taxi; hot wind was blowing newspapers around. We drove along avenues that steadily ascended, grew steadily shadier; and I was, all at once, stricken by nostalgia — for right here where I was, for other times here, for myself when little. A green lawn where I once played with a girl named Astrid; a brownstone château behind curly iron gates, lovely, cool, superb, long lost . . . I could have wept at being back.

We have arrived. My mother is paying off the cab, while cries of greeting come from those hurrying down the concrete walk. My grandmother in black brocade, wearing her tortoise-shell cross, trotting in little satin slippers . . . My aunt, with curly golden hair, a radiant smile. . . . The doctor, tall, red-haired, mustached, wearing his white flannel trousers from tennis. Back on the screened porch the baby rocks her carriage back and forth and croaks with excitement.

As soon as we were shown to our rooms my mother used to lie down, worn out from the trip. I issued forth, to admire once more the specialties of the house: teakwood doors and moldings, Chinese antiquities brought home by the doctor's missionary brother, gold tea-paper on the living-room walls. The house was full of treasures and of life. Somebody opens the front door and ripples out, "Anybody home?" It is Cousin Helen from down the street, come to say how glad she is we've come. Nobody ever dropped into *our* house. . . . The telephone rings and my aunt answers it. "Hold the line, please, the doctor's right here." My uncle's voice, calm and authoritative: "Dr. Littell speaking." A maid goes in and out from the kitchen; an embroidered cloth is on the dining-room table.

"Wash your hands, dear," somebody says, and "Run and call your mother." Here in the bosom of her beginnings my mother's lassitudes were understood. *Exertion always taxes*

Lily. . . . My father, on the contrary, never understood them
— he was either defeated or alarmed, and wanted to call a
doctor. He once told me that when they were on their wedding trip to France, and he took her on a long walk at Giverny to see some old painting haunt, she simply gave out at
the walk's farthest reach, and had to recline on a bench
while he went to find a carriage.

Roast beef . . . roasted potatoes. . . . A cool breeze off the
Hudson ruffles the slender flames of the candles that light up
Canton china of which my aunt is inordinately proud: my
mother — a real artist! — admires it. Then the moment has
come; in from the kitchen the maid bears a great, funnel-
shaped mold of peach ice cream with a little round button
at top. Taking my generous-sized silver spoon in hand, I em-
bark upon my helping. We must always have had fresh
peach ice cream, the first night of those arrivals. . . .

. . . I had been asleep. Here in Venice it was almost nine
in the morning; I rolled over. My mother's head was turned
away so that the bones and tendons of her face and neck
were revealed and I could see, not for the first time, that she
was, not just a handsome old lady of eighty-three, but per-
manently, structurally beautiful.

When she felt me looking at her my mother turned over;
my eyes met her gray ones. "Well, where do we begin?"
she said briskly.

I could not have been more astonished.

I think that all of us felt buoyed up on Venice, like the gon-
dolas on the glassy lagoon, as we walked down the *calle*
after breakfast, across the tiny bridge, past shopwindows
filled with queer specialties — men's wooden coat-stands, I

remember, by the dozen — to get to the Accademia. The quality of the light that fell on the enormous pictures inside seemed, itself, large, grand and Italian. At noon we came out and crossed over what our friend told us used to be called the Iron Bridge when she was a girl visiting her uncle in his palazzo on the Grand Canal. You went up steps high above the Grand Canal and down the other side; the only place except the Rialto, she told us, where you could cross by anything but *traghetto* — gondola-ferry. All her information seemed fascinating, fresh.

On the other side a sun-filled *campo* was as livable as a large, square sitting room. We sat at a table just out of reach of the sun, and drank Punt e Mes vermouth. The place was too good to leave, and we stayed and had lunch. Suddenly my mother didn't like the food. It seemed to her foreign in the wrong sense. I could not bear for anything to break the sunny spell. "The food is wonderful," I told her sternly, as if she were my little girl. "Real Italian cuisine."

Was it that afternoon (it could have been, the way my mother kept right on going) or another that we walked all the way to the Piazza — in one end of its vast elegance and out the other — to see the Carpaccio exhibition at the Ducal Palace? It fits in with that first-day mood; the sense of floating one often has, in Venice, on a crystalline, faintly reverberating pink glass sea. I think in fact we probably went back to the *pensione* after the slight disillusionment at lunchtime. In the middle of the day the maid always closed the shutters, so that when we entered our rooms the light was flickering in, cool and green off the water, although the zinnias outside in the garden burned like suns. Most days after lunch we did sleep, like the Italians, and issued forth in the cool of the afternoon to see the sights of Venice.

Whenever it was we went to the Carpaccio show, which my mother was passionately anxious to see, we had to climb several flights of ducal stairs to get to it. Pictures had been assembled from all over the world; there was even a small head of a girl from the Boston Museum, stuck off in a corner. The famous paintings in series were hung so that each series filled an entire room. My mother, looking Edwardian in a broad-brimmed gray felt hat, progressed slowly, slowly, around a room where the sufferings of St. Ursula were displayed.

My friend and I finished with them in no time; I wondered once more what it is artists are looking for when they go up close to a picture, back away, go up close again squinting. After my friend and I had finished the other rooms too, I went to find my mother. She was still there. "Don't you remember," I said, "Papa used to have a joke about St. Ursula. Wasn't there a headmaster of some girls' school, some clergyman Papa used to call St. Ursula and the Eleven Thousand Virgins?"

My mother looked blank. "I don't know what you're talking about," she said. She was off in the world of painting — a world my father would have understood but I didn't. I felt left out, almost the way I used to when, after supper at home, my mother and father would embrace; I never could bear it until I had horned in. I wandered off to look at pictures more interesting to me — a Christ lying dead in Golgotha with three vacant crosses tiny on a hillside in the distance; a small painting of merry Venetian prostitutes with sly eyes and lascivious lips. It seemed strange for me to be the one waiting for my mother to get tired and go home, instead of the other way around. . . .

. . . In the thirty years since my father died I had found, trying to carry out the responsibility I felt I inherited from him for keeping my mother up and out, that the surest lure to effort was always to remind her of things he'd done. Sheer longing, coupled with unreasonable remorse for what she considered ways she failed him, had made her change many of her habits to his, like getting up early in the morning. I am sure my father was the reason she agreed to come to Italy.

"Your father was so *tremendously* informed on art," she was forever crying when I would have tea with her in the apartment, after she came to live near me in Virginia. "And I'm so ignorant! *He* saw all the great paintings. When he was in Paris and had almost no money he *still* managed to get to the Prado more than once. And to Holland. And Venice. Think of all those Titians and Tintorettos and Veroneses! Venice is full of them, and I've never even been to Italy!" One afternoon I said, "All right, let's *go* to Italy."

Once having had the idea, I was too pleased with it to take no for an answer when my mother developed qualms about going so far away, with Aunt Nancy, now a widow, lying in a Minnesota nursing home. We had booked passage on a ship, but I explained to my mother about jet speed. "In case of emergency, you always could get home," I said. My mother's forever-young eyes stared at the idea of six hundred miles an hour. "I can't imagine it," she declared. "—I don't think I want to go to Italy anyhow. I'm too old for all that rushing around."

"Oh, Mother," I said. (The time never comes when one is too old to say "Oh, Mother.") "We're not going to do any rushing around."

When I told my husband that my mother almost backed out of the trip, he said, "Don't forget the world is a jungle, to Lily." And a professor friend, one of my mother's greatest admirers, threw a jolt into me by remarking, "I hope you're not pushing your mother into too much. It would be awful if she died on the trip." I myself could not but consider what seemed a real likelihood, that she might become too exhausted to continue the journey. I remembered that walk my parents started out on, long ago on their honeymoon.

Then my mother seemed to surrender to the idea of the trip. That summer on Cape Ann before we sailed, she turned casual about locking doors, after a lifetime of being inordinately cautious. It was a relief, when I came up from swimming, not to have to knock and call to get into the house. She even agreed to leave the house open for my son to close later when we were abroad, when she had never before let anyone but herself close the house, and often said young people have no judgment. Just before we sailed she had to go to my dentist. I was in the room when she telephoned for an appointment. "This is Nancy Hale's daughter," she began, and then corrected herself. I'd felt as if I were holding one of a little girl's hands to lead her abroad, while my father held on to the other. . . . Yet here I was in Venice, actually having to kill time at the Carpaccio show because my mother wasn't in the least ready to go home.

After two weeks we went on to Rome's gloomy magnificence. Living at a hotel near the via Veneto, we went walking in the Borghese Gardens under the vast umbrella pines — heavy, almost black — overhanging a mournful little carrousel. I feared Rome would depress my mother — always so prone to melancholy — but not at all; her new energy never flagged. After one full day at the Vatican and the Vatican Gardens, I expressed my astonishment to our friend. She said, "Some people do get a big lift out of traveling."

"But you don't understand," I said. "She never got a lift out of traveling. She never wanted to go anywhere!"

"She *looks* strong," my friend said, as if she doubted my word.

"All her strength always went into her painting," I said. "When my father died, all she felt for him went into it, too."

One burning noontime my mother and I were trapped in the Piazza di Spagna after seeing Keats's rooms — every taxi taken at that hour. We could have sat on a bench in the little park, we could have lunched at one of the restaurants in the Foreigners' Quarter; instead my mother elected to climb the Spanish Steps, which made a shortcut to our hotel. When we reached a landing I at last persuaded her to sit down on a parapet. "Now look here," my mother said. "You need never worry about my heart, if that's what you're exercised over. I have an exceptional heart." It was absurd how relieved I felt.

Later that afternoon, when we were taking our siestas, I remembered how magnificently my mother had been able to sail through the death of her own mother, only a year after my father died. At the time I was far from impressed; I tend-

ed to watch my mother with a sternly critical eye. At any ex-
cess of feeling, any hint of collapse, I was ready with brisk
words to rally and admonish. I wanted my mother to live
up to my father's standards of courage and endurance. Tears,
for instance, were *out*. . . .

My grandmother had fallen and broken her hip at the age
of eighty-seven, and was bedridden for months, in the same
room where she had always slept on her visits to us, in a
maple double bed. Now she lay in a narrow bed, easier to
make with my grandmother in it. After she became delirious, a wooden plank barred the side open to the room, so
she could not fall out. Some unsolved life problem gripped
her, and she became a very little girl sitting with her sister
in some railroad station of the 1860's, waiting for their hellfire-preaching father to come and fetch them. "Father, where
are you?" called the agitated little voice from the upstairs
bedroom. "Julia and I have been waiting so long!"

With a start I woke and turned over on the bed in the darkened Roman hotel room. "Auntie Jule" died long, long
ago, before I was even born. . . .

. . . After my grandmother died, my uncle and Aunt
Nancy took my mother on a motor trip. Paradoxically, un-
reasonably, I even viewed that well-meant activity with a
sternly critical eye too, for my attitude to my aunt and
uncle was colored by memories of the passionate home-
sickness I used to suffer on those childhood visits to them,
after my mother left me and went home.

The summer had come when we returned together from
a New York visit a day early, to find what remained my
childhood's nightmare — my father gone. He did not get

home until after midnight: My mother discovered he had been reduced to such pitiful expedients as breakfasting on cold cereal with water on it, because the milkman failed him. She vowed that never again would she leave my father alone to suffer. She used to leave my aunt's after a couple of days' visit, abandoning me. After she had gone, almost at once, mysteriously and drastically the visits began to go bad.

"Goodmorninggoodmorninggoodmorning," carols the doctor as he descends the stairs to breakfast with a springy tread. Sun glistens on the shiny bristles of his mustache. Simultaneously my father remarks in my ear, "Good old Elgin." The doctor's name was Elton, but it was typical of my father's private sense of humor that to call him "Elgin" sounded insulting, although to nobody but himself — which, of course, included me. He had never been able to get over the time he heard the doctor greet my mother, "Well, Lilian, how's art?"

My aunt, in those days, was in stages of giving up art; in her case the violin. Sometimes she would practice — high stringed notes nostalgic and sweet in the morning sunshine — while as of yore my grandmother accompanied her on the piano, but all around were distractions. In-laws were forever dropping in, warm, importunate, and fond. There were the delightful busynesses of housewifery. "I implore you not to forsake your instrument," my grandmother would say in her sharp, irritating voice — at least it irritated my father. "Think of all I sacrificed for you to become a violinist of concert caliber!" In my ear my father said, "Quite so, dear lady." It was another insult that hurt nobody. My grandmother simply loved to be called "dear lady."

Then my aunt would practice again; but all around was life. After years of deprivation there was the darling baby — oh, joy! The darling baby, whom I was sent to push in her perambulator down gloomy avenues, up mournful boulevards, screamed when she wanted to go one way and I went another. "Curious, how adoption needn't preclude a family likeness," my father said.

Sometimes, as I sat in one of the green wicker rocking chairs on the piazza of the Tennis Club, watching my uncle bound about the court and listening to the summery ping . . . ping . . . of tennis balls, I had a faint apprehension, like a memory at one remove, of how I might have enjoyed it all; how happy I might have been. Then a fat lady in voile stooped to speak to me. I got up reluctantly and kicked the ground behind me in lieu of a curtsy. "So this is Little Nancy. Just like your auntie!" she said. I scowled. I was not like my auntie, I was my father's own child.

"She's a tiny bit homesick," my aunt murmured, apologetically. She was wonderfully sympathetic, considering it was her adored surroundings that so depressed me. "Your mother was always sad too, when she was a little girl," she told me. "Even right there at home with us who loved her. You know what she said when she was about four? She said, 'I don't like it here on earth. I want God to come and take me back.' You're like that, Baby Hale."

"Oh dear," my father said in my ear. Sentimentality distressed him. Personally I felt more frightened. *I* had no wish to die, and it was only here that I felt sad. "I'm *not*," I said furiously. (Later, when I remembered my infant mother's saying, it seemed to me to have been her one act of re-

bellion against her Victorian bringing-up; one of those un-
availing threats to die that little children do make against au-
thority.)

Each summer in the end I was reduced for pleasure to a
few despicable, solitary joys — standing out in the pantry
holding to my nose a loaf of the Graham bread they ate, to
smell its sad, wholesome sweetness; admiring the rows of
cups, banded in deep ruby color, that hung from the glassed-
in pantry shelves. Then I would turn and go out the kitchen
door to my secret hiding place.

It was back of the concrete areaway, with its two large
trash cans. A horse chestnut had been left standing, wedged
between areaway and fence, when they built the house, and
long ago on some former visit I'd excavated in its roots a re-
pository for things like some blue china beads with gold
blobs painted on them that I found in one of the trash cans;
a blue jay's feather, bloody-tipped; the wafer-thin toad that
a truck out in the avenue had run over, still faintly disgusting around the edges. Other magic charms were there,
mysterious and comforting. . . .

. . . When I was sent home at the end of the summer I
could have died of relief. I remember one such evening
with my father and mother working together down in the
lower vegetable garden, in a dusk filled with the autumn
song of insects, while I wander around the terrace under the
lilac trees, their blooms now long and irrevocably gone,
past the trellis where the trumpet vine climbs to my bedroom window. Sometimes I had lain in bed plotting to escape down that trellis. Escape indeed! My throat aches with
finding myself back home alive.

"Saved, as by fire," my father says when he kisses me good-night. I don't know what it means, but it shows he understands. And in the morning I would watch him break his eggs and drink his coffee. "Coffee is the drink of heroes, going off to battle," he used to say. "And tea is the drink of the defeated, coming home at night." When he left, in a great rush of shouting and commotion, I would go up to my mother's room. She sits before the mirror in an embroidered corset-cover, arms raised to brush her long, dark, wavy hair. Everybody is where they belong, everything is safe. It is days before my euphoria subsides and I resume the cares and crosses of an only child — the weight of nations on my head holding the family together, not figuratively but literally, it felt.

It seems as if my father — bursting, soaring out to the studio each morning — might one day fail to come home at all. I am needed at home like an amulet, to ensure his return. Conversely it seems as if my mother has to be kept from sinking forever into the depths of dreams. Her late risings, after I had gone to school . . . her long, long rests in the afternoon . . . her early bedtimes. . . . I am needed at home to keep her up and looking after me. — But I was in Rome, I realized with another start; *I* was, at least in theory, looking after *her*.

One scene that stands out, on that trip of ours to Italy, is the afternoon we met that British celebrity, that baroque survival of high-life naughtiness, Norah Grimsby; said to have been the mistress of certain kings. On the last leg of our journey we came to Florence, where our traveling companion, who had known the lady in Paris, insisted that meeting

Mrs. Grimsby was an experience I mustn't miss; my mother, she added, could at least enjoy the gardens. She took us to where Mrs. Grimsby lived, on a sort of country estate within the Florentine city limits. Seven acres of rolling woodland and gardens surrounded a Quattrocento palace, three of its stories rented to rich Americans. Mrs. Grimsby lived, among photographs and mementos of her flamboyant past, on the *piano nobile.*

She kept us waiting ten minutes in the salon before she tottered in, tiny, rouged, and shrill, kissing our friend and inquiring after various international characters before greeting us. I had time to hope that the gardens really were good; it seemed the meeting of two hostile worlds when they finally shook hands—that ancient harridan in her fashionably brief frock, and my mother wearing her broad-brimmed gray hat, her face as innocent and earnest as a young girl's.

The fact was she and Mrs. Grimsby hit it off instantly. I could not have been more astonished, as we walked through the extensive grounds, to hear them chattering together faster and faster, like old cronies. "B.B. said he fancied this garden most," the old creature rattled on. "He *would,* would he not? I call it bleak, m'self. B.B. could be a bit too-too!" "I met Mr. Berenson once at dinner at Mrs. Gardner's in Boston," my mother replied, with animation. After a while the two elderly ladies turned back to the palazzo, announcing they were going to start their tea alone. When we entered the salon a little later, it was evident they had been talking a mile a minute. They broke off when we came in.

When my mother and I were getting undressed for bed

that night I said, "You always had a fit if *I* told the kind of story Mrs. Grimsby tells."

My mother stared. "What's Mrs. Grimsby got to do with you?" she said.

"Just you always correct me if I say so much as God-damn," I said.

"How are you going to know I'm your mother if I don't correct you?" she said.

There seemed nothing to say. As we were getting into bed I added, "I just never knew you approved of Mrs. Grims-by's kind of person."

"I don't know what you mean, kind of person," my mother said. "Mrs. Grimsby and I have a great deal in common."

"What, for heaven's sake?"

"Well, she's my age, for one thing," my mother retorted. "And for another, we agree that your generation can be aw-fully stuffy."

I put out the light. Lying in the darkness I reflected, calm-ing myself, that I would never be able to understand my mother if she lived to be a hundred. . . .

. . . As with those illnesses of hers, in my childhood, that she seemed almost to enjoy — as though, I sometimes thought after I grew up, they had been an escape from something far more menacing than illness. When *I*, as a child, had a fever, I found it most unpleasant; the faces of the kings and queens on the playing cards with which my mother sought to amuse me turned sly and ferret-like. But whenever my mother was in bed with a fever she smiled, blissfully engrossed else-where.

Once when I visited her, soon after the death of my grandmother, she told me about a recent, severe bout of influenza (actually her only suggestion of collapse after her life's two major losses, for all my apprehensions). The doctor had insisted upon a practical nurse. "She was a nice, homely old thing," my mother said. "But do you know, when I was sickest, she looked perfectly beautiful. *Everything* looked beautiful. My bedroom was draped in rich, ruby-colored hangings, and the nurse was wearing a brocade dress with panniers, like a lady at the French court. It was all so much nicer than the way it really is!"

. . . I turned over in the Florentine bed; the sound of late traffic on the via Tornabuoni returned to my ears. After *I* was very ill, on the contrary, in my middle years, and came up to my mother's house beside the sea to recuperate, it was the being out and in the world again that felt like an escape.

My uncle and Aunt Nancy were there on a visit too. They used to ask me to join them in a nightly game of cribbage at the dining-room table after supper. She lame now, he after two heart attacks, they had passed long and useful lives. Their graying blond heads shine like old gold under the lamp set on the sill of the open window. A June bug or two bangs against the screen; and as we play we hear the bell buoy rock and ring from far away across the summer sea.

Nothing any more conceals from me how pleasant they are, how nice to be with, how good. The twenty-five years since my father died has finally separated us enough so that I can see it was not I who had to fight a world that seemed to be saying art does not matter. It was not I whose wife's family exercise over her an influence toward prudery. As I in-

sert a peg into a hole in the cribbage board, it dawns on me
— there in the afternoon of my life — that my childhood's
great anxiety was only nightmare; my father never had the
slightest intention of leaving us. The gusto of his morning de-
partures were simply that it took him a major head of steam
to go out and meet a world like that. I knew plenty of people whose childhoods really were broken; but *my* father
stayed. He kept my childhood whole the way the skin seals
up the body, waiting till I was grown up to die.

"Will you discard, Little Nancy?" my uncle says. I smile
back at the friendly face — my life's first image of the outside, non-art world. Plain fact seems to receive me with
open arms, a voice break in — "This is your announcer, returning you to reality . . ."

. . . After three weeks in Florence we separated from our
traveling companion, who was remaining in Europe. On
the boat going home I used to wake up in the berth that
faced my mother's end to end, bracing my legs on the sides
against the increasingly violent motion of the vessel. It is always a letdown to come home from any journey — or *I*
have always found it so. My mother, however, had announced her intention of flying to Minneapolis to see Aunt
Nancy as soon as we landed. It appeared she had already arranged the whole thing through letters without saying a
word to me. My cousin was flying on from St. Paul to es-
cort her back. I used to lie in bed and reflect what a pity it
was: all those years my mother had had it in her to go to
those places and do those things. We could perfectly well
have taken this trip long ago. It was as if she had never
availed herself of a whole, outer dimension.

At some time, however (was it one morning in bed, or later?—one quality of recollection is to scramble the sequence of events that are associated), it came to me that, earlier in her life, my mother could not have done it. Just as, after my father died, new strengths came into her painting to transform it, just so the heights of activity and new tolerance she scaled in Italy were like the same strengths at last made flesh; as though act blossomed out of idea as naturally as flower from seed. I remembered my father, how he used to say, "Art first, life afterward." It seemed to me that in my mother's love affair with his memory, her effort to redeem the ways she felt she had failed him, the last had ended by becoming first and the first last. The Victorian little girl had finally capitulated to my father and to me, and to a world where sadness, for a state of being, is not a working word, a word no longer in use. She had come out of her life's shell, and for a second I had the dizzying fancy that the sky was now the limit.

After breakfast in our berths, I used to go to the dancing lessons I signed up for the first day out; at home I seldom get the opportunity to dance. In the smoking room aft, a group of middle-aged men and women, staggering against the ship's motion, were put through their paces. "One — two — cha-cha-cha," droned Tony LaTouche, the instructor, in a Brooklyn accent. He was middle-aged too, but different — dry-skinned, lean, balancing to the roll and pitch like a gull sliding down wind currents.

The storm was growing worse; I never saw such waves. The ship banged, wrenched itself to one side, straightened out, pounded down from monstrous heights, shivered in all its length, began to bang again. My mother felt mildly queasy and remained in bed. Two days out from New York, when I went to my dancing lesson, half the group was absent; the rest looked apprehensive or dogged. Only Tony remained as though impermeable to nature; fleshless, smoking innumerable cigarettes — the professional *artiste,* unmoved by hope or fear. "You're a nice little dancer," he said, after choosing me to exhibit with him the complete routine. I felt irrationally flooded with gratitude. A fat woman fell down at that point and had to be helped to her feet. "Our time's up," Tony said.

I decided to sit down and watch the couple who followed us every day. They were late, and Tony waited near my chair, flicking ashes from his cigarette into an ashtray he held; I kept imagining like some eager insecure girl that he would ask me to dance again. Then the couple came through the glass doors, looking as though their night had been of the hardest "Okay, Mr. and Mrs. Harlan, let's go," Tony said, turning on the record.

What was so queer in the atmosphere? It wasn't only the storm. There was something macabre about the record pattering on:

> *. . . the bossa nova,*
> *The da-ance of love . . .*

Harlan, in Glen plaid, danced face to face with his wife in her chic print, gazing into her eyes. Their faces were immobile, their bodies controlled, their rhythm perfect. "Let's take it over," Tony said, setting the needle back. From standing as though mesmerized, the Harlans resumed their stealthy, catlike steps. Tony smoked a cigarette and watched them critically. He set the needle back again:

> Dance the bossa nova,
> The da-ance of love.

Why did something irreparable seem about to happen? I swallowed to test my throat; perhaps I was catching something. I got up and left, stumbling as I crossed the companionway, where you could smell the ozone. On the bulletin board next to color photographs of passengers in evening dress smiling up from their dinner tables, and a notice of to-day's movie showing, new posters were tacked up giving instructions for landing procedures in New York. In the lounge four or five people sat leafing nervously through copies of *Country Life.* One woman was wearing an orange life jacket.

When I got back to our stateroom I told my mother, who was still resting, about the landing instructions. Then I asked her again whether she really wanted to fly to Minnesota. "It'll be a jet, you know," I reminded her.

"I don't care. I have to go and see Nancy," she said. She turned her face away toward the porthole, and I could see the indestructibly beautiful bones and tendons of her face and throat.

After lunch I tried to take a nap, and then went to the four o'clock movie. When I came back to our stateroom again, my mother was sitting bolt upright on the edge of her berth, fully dressed in suit and topcoat, a black felt sailor hat pinned to the top of her white hair. "Where have you been?" she exclaimed when she saw me, and sprang to her feet. "I thought you were never coming!"

"I went to the movie," I said. "Don't you remember?"

"Wandering off without telling anyone where you are when we have to get off this ship!"

"Dear," I said. "Not today."

"But you *said* . . ." The confidence was seeping out of her voice. "I distinctly heard you say we were to go ashore."

"Day after tomorrow," I said. "Not today. Two whole days from now."

My mother sat down. After a minute she reached up her arms and unpinned her hat. Then she reached over to the built-in dressing table for the clothes brush, and began to brush the black felt.

We spent one night in New York, then I took my mother out to the airport. As we approached my cousin from opposite ends of a great, glacial hall, my mother held out both hands and exclaimed, "We've been on the most wonderful trip!"

I glanced at her to see if her spirits really were that high, and her face was illumined — definitely, unmistakably — with the light I had seen in it before, when somewhere in her depths new visual plots were hatching.

After I kissed her at the gate, I was left in a tearing hurry to get home, like an animal heading for its hole. It was natural enough, I had been abroad so long; however, after I had been away from my mother for a few hours the feeling wore off. I had hardly started putting the house back in shape, and had not even unpacked, when my cousin telephoned from Minnesota. My mother had suffered a coronary conclusion — sort of; not exactly. . . .

"Shall I come?" I asked the doctor whose telephone number my cousin gave me.

"No indeed!" he said briskly. "We caught it so early we don't expect it to amount to a thing."

I telephoned to the room at a hospital where my mother had been taken. Her voice was blurred with sedatives. "What do you know about that?" she murmured. "I didn't know I *could* get anything wrong with my heart."

"I love you to pieces," I said.

"I love *you* to pieces," she replied, sounding cordial but distrait.

Next morning very early the telephone rang. "Well, she didn't make it," my cousin said.

For a long time afterwards I thought my cousin might have chosen some less callous way to tell me. Now it seems to me, however, that she put her finger on exactly the difference from all the other times when, out of my mother's vis-à-vis with, not the world exactly, but her idea of the world resident in my father, she did make some new thing, some work of art.

At first, too, it seemed terrible she'd had to die way out there; away from me, away from home. But then I began to see where home was, for her — not where home is for me. The world that had my father in it constituted, for her, the outside world. Her own parents had a different set of struggles altogether. Perhaps the place she picked to die in came closest, because of my aunt's presence, to what was left of a world my grandmother departed years ago.

When I try to imagine my mother in her last hours, she is lying in a shadowy room, a shadowy bed, drowsy with drugs. A nurse is bending over her, waiting for her to finish talking to me on the telephone; she looks like a French marquise in her panniered, brocade dress. Still another figure hovers in the shadows. I try to visualize her and she looks little and kind and helpful, the way she used to when I was a child and had a stomachache and she would come and lay her warm hand on my middle, easing it as nothing else could.

There is nothing any longer to irritate in that tiny figure. She is not *my* mother-in-law, she is my loving grandmother. I can't see her more clearly than that, though — not the way my mother must have seen her when she was dying, back where all the ladders start. I know, from hearing my mother's voice, that her state was satisfied and engrossed in her own, other, forever unimaginable rag-and-bone shop of the heart.

An Arrangement in Parents

WHEN one is young, rebellion is the need. Anything at all serves as the thing to reject — whatever lies closest to hand, which is likely to be parents. When my own children were struggling to become anything so long as it wasn't me, sometimes in self-defense I used to point out I wasn't what they assumed I was, really. But then I would remember my youth, and that greater service no parent can render than to be rejected. A good parent even becomes whatever rebellion next needs.

Rebellion, in my adolescence, was complicated by the fact that, while my contemporaries were occupied in running away from conventionality, I was perforce running away *to* it. Nothing, I felt, could be more of an embar-

rassment than to have painter parents. I could not imagine
the mother of my school friend Denise — a chic lady who
bought her clothes from Chanel — bending over double to
look at things upside down.

One of the Impressionist painter's problems was managing
to see things as they looked, without getting trapped by
what they were supposed to be. To this end, my parents,
when at work, used various expedients — standing with their
backs to a picture and its model and looking at them through
a hand mirror; or bending over and looking at them sidewise or in reverse. Even when they were out of doors, visibly painting landscape, they went in for this sort of peculiar
behavior.

The only thing that ever kept my father home from his
Boston studio in the daytime was to be at work on a painting of the white hollyhocks in our garden, or of a model in
a veiled hat standing beside his favorite white standard rose
tree, or on one of his all-green pointillist landscapes of mead-
ow and orchard.

I would come out of the house on some hot, murmurous
June morning and see, far out in the green sea of the fields,
a white spot — my father, in battered sola topee and shirt-
sleeves, painting. I would walk down through our orchard,
where I could smell the fruit beginning to form on the early
apple tree, skirt the swamp, and climb the radiant eastern
slope toward Billy Goodwin's Rock. My father sat in full
sun on a campstool, hunched over, in front of a sketching
easel on which his canvas was secured. The kind of enormous oval palette he favored, with a bunch of brushes stuck
in the hole, was over his thumb, and his boxes of paint

tubes and turpentine and linseed-oil bottles lay spread open on the grass.

Just as I was approaching, my father stood up and, in full view of the Goodwins' house, the Sullivans' house, the Neffs' house, set his feet far apart and, leaning over, viewed his picture and the scene between his legs.

"Papa! *Must* you do that?" I hissed. I think of myself as dressed in a beige copy of a Chanel dress, a choker of over-size pearls around my neck, and high heels; not such a slouch at the inappropriate myself.

"I've got to see what that tree by the stream looks like," he explained when he stood up straight again. One good thing about my father was that, working, conversation never bothered him. My father in his studio would entertain models with long stories having complicated points, the working out of which didn't distract his mind a bit. Frequently he burst into song. "It's been getting stupider and stupider looking," he said now.

"It looks like a willow to me," I said.

"If a tree is any good, it ought to look as well upside down as right side up. Better. Because you're not so dead used to it."

"Things have to mean something, to be anything," I instructed him, coldly.

"Don't be hard on the old gentleman, Job Lots," he said.

I froze. It was a humiliating pet name from my infancy.

He threw me an affectionate glance; my expression remained haughty. "'But he forgot and sang "Tra-la-la, The Queen of Lilliput's own Papa!"'" he declaimed. "'She frowned and ordered him off to bed. He said he was sorry.

She shook her head. His clean shirt front with his *tears* was stained,'" he went on, plaintively. "'But discipline *had* to be maintained!'"

How could anyone cope (I had just acquired the word "cope") with frivolity like that? There seemed nothing for it but to stroll indifferently away. As I went, he began to sing at the top of his voice:

"'*What's the matter with Father? He's all right!*'"

Such eccentricities made puzzling the problem of what it was I was rebelling against and for what I pined. I pined for Vionnet blouses, and for gold slave necklaces, and my own stag line at sub-deb parties; for using just the right adjectives of praise, like "divine" and of scorn, like "repulsive," and the right slang, like "nifty." Yet I pined too for the right parents — orthodox ones, against whom I could properly rebel and for the proper reasons.

Sometimes, spending the night with a school friend, my imagination would lead me into creating such parents. "The family's so *stuffy*," I'd say (using just the correct substantive). "They won't let me go to the movies alone with a boy! It's absolutely antediluvian," when, actually, making such a prohibition had never dawned on my parents. Or I might reply, to a question: "Yes, isn't convention loathsome? All those formal tablecloths and stuff the family insists on!" In actual fact, conventional my parents were not; at the time I would have added, "alas."

When my school friends came in turn to spend the night with me, they were often enchanted by what they found. "Your father's so *amusing!*" Denise would exclaim, astonished, and "Your mother's really terribly *attractive!*" I had feared as much. What was disconcerting to a sixteen-year-old was the dim realization — less dim sometimes than others — that my parents, against whom I had every God-given right to rebel, tended to giggle privately about my being the last word in stuffiness myself.

My father's high spirits, his wit and gaiety, never seemed so real to me as after I had left home and gone to live in New York, where I had a job on a magazine devoted to the arts. I used to walk to work in the morning, up Lexington Avenue, feeling as if the lemon-yellow sunshine, the white garbage trucks, the fruit outside the fruit stores, had been created just for me. At the same time I would remember my father and how he said that, back in the days when he was studying under Alden Weir at the Art Students League, he felt as if New York had just been made, that minute, for him. It gave a sort of solidity to my euphoria that my father had felt it before me, and it was one of the ways in which my parents began to rearrange themselves.

My mother, whose perceptions were direct and wordless, had always used my father as her font of artistic wisdom. My father's own life, on the other hand, was devoted to acquiring ever more and more knowledge about art. He was the author of a book on Vermeer, and of columns of newspaper criticism of art. He had read everything, and seemed to remember everything he read, so that to quote, for him, was the natural interlarding of conversation.

In New York, I used him, too; he was my font of conversational stock in trade. At dazzling social moments when my knees shook and my heart quailed, it cut a considerable swathe, with people up to recognizing Vasari, when I could

(having first, of course, built up the gag) quote Paolo Uc-
cello waking his wife up in the middle of the night to say,
"Isn't perspective exciting?" Once I was what I called pet-
rified by a brusque and famous surgeon I sat next to at dinner. He gave me, or so I thought, a surprised, respectful
look when I remarked, "The triceps of the thigh fastens to
the kneecap, and thence, by a tendon, to the tuberosity of
the tibia."

My father himself proved a never-failing subject in making conversation. "When my father was an art student in
Paris in the nineties" was a beginning that caught attention;
there were hundreds of anecdotes, funny or dramatic, I could
follow it up with. My father's aphorisms came off well, too.
"Art first, life afterward" made me sound cynical and experienced. To say things like "My father used to spend the
summers at Giverny, where he knew Monet" helped to
place not so much him as me, I thought — until one afternoon in the office of the magazine where I worked.

The editor, an elderly, well-born dilettante with a nose
for the vogue in art, used to tippet about the various offices
on his painful feet, seeing what was up with us sub-editors.
He liked to stop and tease the secretaries, too, whom he
called by extravagant names: "Elaine the Fair," or "La Prin-
cesse Lointaine." He tried to become one of us — gossiping
about the latest mot of Cocteau or Dorothy Parker or Stra-
vinsky, until an appointment or the telephone would call
him back to his interior-decorated office. The idea was to
make the atmosphere of the office democratic — the democ-
racy of the arts.

I was running on, as usual, about my father. "My father

was over there in Paris about fifteen years, and when he came home he was on top of the heap. He was one of the first Impressionists to hit America."

"Oh?" the editor said. In his eyes — blue, urbane, filled with the goodwill of the completely self-assured — I stared straight at the truth he knew so well. My father was not, ever, at the top of the heap; he was one of the first but never one of the famous American Impressionists. He had never been a success; never.

The editor's private secretary appeared in the doorway. "Mrs. Delano is on the telephone," she told him. The editor tippeted away; but I had looked at the world's view, and despair.

Some months later I lost my job on that magazine. It was for flattering reasons — the rest of the staff said either they or I must go, since I was younger, made more money, and came in later than anybody else — and the reaction to it didn't hit me till late that night.

I had been to a theater and dancing at the nightclub the Algonquin used to operate, with a tall, pock-marked writer who was a good dancer. At my apartment he came in for a nightcap. I made him a drink and carried it to him; when I stood in front of him holding out the glass, he took it away from me and set it on a table, meaning to kiss me. But, in his arms, instead of kissing him I burst into tears.

I cried a long time; it must have appalled him. I cried at first because the people at the office didn't want me, because of failure; but I cried ultimately — then and after the man had left — thinking of how my father felt, how he had always felt. It seemed to me that night the truth was he hadn't

really been gay or lighthearted at all. He'd put it on to endure failing at the only thing he wanted to be — a successful
painter. And he wasn't; no matter how he tried, no matter
how he drew and drew till the early hours of every morning, no matter how he painted daily, rain or shine.

My mother was always successful — success came to her at
the very start. When she was old and her work finally went
out of fashion, she said to me, "I always took it for granted,
being successful. I assumed I always would be." But my father only got enough encouragement — a popular prize at
one exhibition, a portrait commission resulting from another
— to keep his hopes titillated, and add to his inability to accept reality. He could have immortalized himself as a critic
of art, but he thought nothing of writing — to his family
writing came easy. He did immortalize himself as a teacher.
But that was not what he wanted, either. Nothing mattered
but the coming true of the dreams of his youth when, coming home from the ateliers, New York seemed born specially
for him.

The editor of the magazine that fired me used to say,
"One *does* so wonder why anybody ever paints an allegorical
picture." Toward the end of his life my father did paint allegorical pictures, against all his artistic principles. One, I remember, was of a group of huge, surging, tossing horses on
a beach, reined in by their naked rider. One was of a winged
centaur, fabulous, soaring against a crimson-streaked dark
sky while, far below on earth, stands the tiny relentless figure of the archer who has loosed the arrow that has struck
the centaur's flank to bring him down. Another is of a nude —
like a wraith, like a muse — hair spread out in the water on

which she floats, drifting down a stream among water lilies by moonlight; she is, perhaps, dead.

Such pictures will always be unsalable. They belied, moreover, every tenet of painting in which my father believed—being of imaginary subjects, not painted from the model, nor demonstrating the composition of light. They lacked everything except meaning, secret and protean meaning; the meanings of a literary mind, to which, in the end, he must have been driven.

My father died in Boston when I was twenty-three, of a ruptured appendix from which he suffered terribly, my mother told me afterward, but for which he refused to have a doctor until it was too late, for fear a doctor would somehow stop him from working. When I went up from New York to the undertaker's chapel funeral, I could feel—sitting between my mother and my professor uncle—nothing but the sorrow and the waste of his life. My uncle read aloud some poetry—the only service there was:

> *He has outsoared the shadow of our night;*
> *Envy and calumny and hate and pain*
> *And that unrest which men miscall delight*
> *Can touch him not and torture not again. . . .*

The dry, academic voice ceased; the undertaker's men began shepherding us up toward the coffin. Nobody had thought to tell them not to leave it open. Nobody had the spirit to resist now. We filed past, and when it was my turn to look at my father, the shock was nightmarish—his face was gray, the color of clay.

The catastrophe which separated my parents separated them for me, too. I remembered my father as alone, en-

during his tragedy — a pain he hid from my mother, I realized, or expressed only in ways like those paintings,
disguised perhaps even from himself. I thought of him long
ago, when he would sit with my mother beside the fire and
read aloud after dinner. He loved the early Yeats, and I
used to love to hear him read it, but now I interpreted it differently:

> *She bade me take life easy, as the grass grows on the weirs;*
> *But I was young and foolish, and now am full of tears.*

In the years following his death, my mother could never
understand why I didn't want to talk about my father, as I'd
once loved to do, when we would tell each other his jokes
and repeat his badinage.

"But your father loved you so!" she would say, distressed.
"Why do you close up so when I mention him? Don't you
love him any more? He loved *you*. When you were a baby,
and he played with you, he was the happiest man I ever
saw. He used to say a rhyme — 'All my fancy Dwells on
Nancy. . . .'"

But short of tempests of tears, which I spared her, there
was no way I could express what I felt about my father. For
all those long years after his death, he was as though cut off.
There *were* no happy thoughts to think about him. My father was alone in the shades, walking disconsolate, forever
longing and forever thwarted.

My mother never stopped singing his praises. When she
was an old lady, people used to comment on how she talked
of him as though he had died only yesterday. She spoke
with ever fresh enthusiasm for his wit and wisdom; with almost girlish awe for his achievement. Sometimes I felt im-

patient with her. "What's the use of dwelling on the past?" I said once. "You have to live in reality. People that are gone are gone — they're not even ghosts."

"I wish your father *would* come back as a ghost," she said once. "I'd love it."

When she died, I couldn't mourn her. She was too full of years, she'd expressed herself in her work too completely, to mourn. But as she sank back into the ground of the past, gradually she seemed to join my father, dead for so long, in the heaven of my recollection. Gradually, close to her, his lonely sorrows seemed to drift away, like snowbanks in the morning. Now that they were both dead, they seemed to move into a world they really did inhabit — their world as I knew it, not as I feared it to be.

I am sick with measles, and the shades are drawn because my eyes are sensitive to light. All afternoon my mother sits in the upstairs hall outside my open door, reading *The Dove in the Eagle's Nest* aloud. Twilight comes. My father gets home from his studio, stamping the snow off in the hall downstairs, but more quietly than usual because I am ill, and then comes upstairs to pay me a visit before supper is served.

"How is my suffering cat?"

The evening passes, and the sound of waltzes and ma- zurkas, all played at a deliberate tempo, drifts up the stairs. In the latter half of his life my father learned to play the piano, and used after dinner to read from albums of Cho- pin, accurately but very slowly. The sounds of home shutting up for the night drift up along with the music to me — the brass lock of the front door being turned, the sound of the fire irons in the living room as the logs are pulled apart.

"Get up and brush your teeth, darling," my mother comes and says. Later she lays her cool hand on my forehead. My father stands in the doorway to say goodnight too; she gets up from my bedside and goes and stands beside him, with her arms up over his shoulders; she used to drape herself on him.

"My little spotted pard," my father says.

I attempt a joke. "Pardner?"

"No. A mythological cat with spots. Like you."

Then they have gone. Later there comes another sound — my father's big chair from his study, the one with the wide, swinging arm on which he can lay his work, bumping against the banisters as he drags it upstairs to set in my room. When I was specially sick, my father used to spend the night sitting up in my room in case I should wake and need something.

He leaves it there and goes away to work downstairs, on his drawing or his studies. But when I wake in the night I feel him there, and sometimes see him, silhouetted against the gray early light from around the shades, sleeping in his big chair. He wakes at six so as to get to the studio, and when I myself wake it is to hear him singing in his tub:

> *Oh, it's time to get up in the morning,*
> *Hooray, hooray, hooray!*

Sometimes, when I am going to sleep at night, I walk through the rooms of the house where I grew up and where they are reunited, enjoying the effects my mother's taste created — a fluted white china teapot (broken in a dozen places and mended with white lead; she was always saving) that stands on the broad sill of the west window in the dining room, between dark-blue-and-white glazed chintz curtains she made herself. Or I wander into my father's study, where I can view the things he needed in the evenings to work with —Dunlop's *Anatomy,* Elie Faure, Bridgman's *Book of a Hundred Hands,* as well as piles of copper plates and the diamond or ruby points he used for drawing on them, jars filled with Venus pencils, and the little bottles of India ink, and pens, with thin metal handles, to use it with: all objects real as real and true as true.

Perhaps it is extravagant to imagine that they are only upstairs, snickering together the way they always did, at convention and the world's ways; but for me it seems less of an extravagance than a preservation to imagine they are somewhere. Perhaps in the garden. Not the same thing as, but indistinguishable from, the rose tree and its standard, he stands, an unyielding, indispensable support, for her to spill over; like roses. There they entwine in a true lover's knot, for true lovers all to admire.